VANESSA JOY
EDUCATION

BUILDING AND MARKETING YOUR WEDDING BUSINESS

By Vanessa Joy

Table of Contents

PART - 1 | BUILDING YOUR BUSINESS — 5

How to Make Your Side Hustle Your Full-Time Work and Quit Your Day Job! — 6
The Time to Change Things Up — 11
Organizing for Efficiency — 17
Perfecting Your Workflow — 24
Outsourcing — 28
Wowing Your Clients — 52
Boosting Your Income — 57
Running Your Studio — 72
Cultivating Your Support Network — 86
Long-Term Plans — 90

PART - 2 | BRANDING YOUR BUSINESS — 99

Getting Back on Track — 100
Social vs. Market Norms: How Treating Your Clients and Employees Defines Your Business — 104
3 Must-have Social Media Tips — 110
4 Steps to Updating Your Social Media Strategy — 114
Secret Methods to Brand Your Business — 116

VANESSA JOY
EDUCATION

Branding for High-End Weddings	127
The Evolution of a Brand	130
How to Clean Up Your Brand in 4 Easy Steps	133

PART - 3 | MARKETING YOUR BUSINESS   137

Compounding Your Efforts for Success, Part 1	138
Compounding Your Efforts for Success, Part 2	142
Instagram Growth: 5 Tips on Getting Your Engagement and Numbers Up	146
Marketing to Millennials	150
5 Social Media Marketing Myths	154
Shake It Up - How to Keep from Marketing Stagnation	159
The 6 Steps to Social Media Marketing Your Weddings	164

PART 1

Building Your Business

How to Make Your Side Hustle Your Full-Time Work and Quit Your Day Job!

I have two businesses, working in both online education and as a wedding event photographer. I love my work - it's definitely a dream job for me. I also make fantastic money from it: more than six figures from each side of the business in net, after-expenses, yearly pay.

Compare that to the day job I used to work, earning $42,000 a year as a Spanish teacher. I've been able to do more of what I love and make much more money doing it. I won't lie, though. It took time--more time than you might think.

I want to share the strategy you can use to take your side hustle and grow it enough to quit your day job. If you follow these steps, you'll be prepared for the challenges of self-employment so that you can also reap the rewards of owning your own business (or two!). Here are the steps to take.

STEP 01 — DON'T JUST QUIT! WORK AT BOTH AT FIRST

I won't lie, you'll probably be working nights and weekends during this stage, but that's the "side" part of having a side hustle. What is so valuable about keeping the security of your day job while you work your side hustle is that you get to test out your skills in the marketplace, but you aren't taking on as much risk as those who just quit their jobs and start from scratch.

Your side hustle will teach you a ton of things about what doesn't work and what does work, but the goal is to start growing your income in that side hustle until it is enough to replace all your income from your day job.

Many people are tempted to get the money from their side work and fold it into the monthly budget, but if you are serious about making the leap to full-time work, don't do it! Keep your expenses as close to the same as possible, using your day income. Put all the side hustle money aside. When they are roughly equal, you switch. Start living off the side hustle money and put your whole-day job paycheck into savings.

This sounds ambitious, but remember, you'll prove to yourself that you can make it when you switch to your side hustle full-time. Don't quit yet either, just because you hit a month that is equal to your day job pay. Instead, keep building that savings account until it equals 3-6 months of expenses. Include everything, too. If your current job has nice perks like insurance or a 401(K) match, you'll want to account for that in your savings.

When you've done that, though, it's time to get started!

STEP 02   SET UP HELPFUL BANK ACCOUNTS

You can make these accounts any time after you know you're getting serious, but definitely set them up before you make the leap and quit your day job. Having your bank accounts in order will help you have a professional, functional structure from the very start!

The biggest reason to have plenty of structure In your finances is that your gross income (everything your side business makes) isn't the same as your net income (what you get to spend personally after all your expenses and taxes). You need a structure that helps you pay taxes, employees, contractors, and other costs before you start thinking of the money as "your paycheck." This helps you avoid getting a huge bill that your business isn't equipped to pay.

- Get a business checking account. Ideally, this will be the place where your clients pay you. Get an account with a bank that doesn't charge fees for having a low balance or for having multiple checking accounts so that you can get organized without worrying about being charged when an account is low.

- Start a payroll expenses checking account. This helps you get organized so that all of your payroll expenses from a given job are covered.

- Start a tangible cost of sales checking account. These are all the expenses you know you'll have to make in order to fulfill an order. In my case, I know that every wedding photography job will involve the expense of creating a physical album, so I always put those costs right into the tangible cost of sales checking account so that I have them handy when I need to pay for the album.

- A taxes checking account is also a good idea. You actually pay quite a bit of taxes on your income at a day job, but it comes out without you handling it yourself, so it's easy to ignore. I recommend putting about 30% of everything that comes into your business into this checking account. You may qualify to pay less, but it's much better to be able to write your checks for quarterly income taxes from this account than to have to scramble in your personal account to find that money.

- An optional fund or checking account would be a sinking fund. When you know you want a big expense in the future, this fund lets you save up for that item over time. I might save up for a new camera in the sinking fund, a little bit each time I'm paid so that it doesn't feel as overwhelming when that expense needs to happen!

I'm particularly indebted to Dave Ramsey's financial advice. I learned much of what helped me create this structure from him. I also learned a lot from Jordan Page, who has suggested a variety of checking accounts that you want to have!

STEP 03 — PLANNING FOR GROWTH!

This stage is really about how you'll deal with success, whatever that looks like for you, on a day-to-day basis. It's fun to think high-level and consider what it'd be like to be "successful," but you need to have things like a workflow or a client management system or a day-to-day plan for how you'll do all the work you commit to and do it well enough to make your customers happy. The key is to make a system that works n ow but will also work when you grow.

This might be about outsourcing - what elements will you consider taking out and having someone else do? Pay attention to what elements of your business you don't like or that you aren't good at or efficient in doing. Write these things down. You may have to do them all now, but when you're growing, you may be able to pay someone else to do this work! A big question is whether or not someone would be willing to do this work for less pay than you are doing it now. You are, after all, the CEO, so as you find people and add them to your team, you may contract out elements of the business for less than you make yourself.

Then it's time to research. What items might you outsource, what would they cost in your area or for your needs, and in what order would you like to outsource them? Make a plan for how well your business needs to be doing before you outsource each item. Ideally, your outsourcing frees up your time to do what you do best, what you enjoy most, or what brings in lots of happy clients—ideally, all three!

Also, remember to think of your future retired self! Plan to put aside 15% of your profit per month into a growth mutual fund—there are tons of opinions on how to save for retirement, but that's my benchmark based on Dave Ramsey's recommendations. You want to think these things through as a business owner.

The sky is the limit for your business: don't limit yourself. Down the road, you might, like me, get into the world of online education to teach about the things you enjoy and to diversify your income. There's a lot to learn, but remember: starting your side business on a firm footing is one of the best ways to eventually quit your day job and do what you love full-time!

The Time to Change Things Up

The Five Warning Signs

We all get in ruts — creatively and motivationally. We can just plain burn out. Sometimes these ruts are phases that pass or the result of spending far too much time comparing oneself to another colleague's highlight reels on Facebook and Instagram. After all, as Theodore Roosevelt said, "Comparison is the thief of joy." We know it's pretty easy to get into a rut that way. But occasionally these ruts are trying to tell us something, and they shouldn't just be ignored, swept under the rug, or hidden behind a smile. Sometimes a rut can turn into a pit if you're not careful.

There are various types of ruts you can fall into that indicate you need a change of pace. Sometimes it's a small change in your workflow or pricing structure that makes all the difference. Other times it's a big change that may affect your career on a larger scale. The key is to identify what kind of rut you're in so that you can work your way out to make a change. Here are five warning signs that you're due for a change and some ways to figure out what your first steps to change should be.

Warning Sign – 01

You're Not Getting Any New Work

———————————

This warning sign can most certainly be an indicator of a number of issues, but primarily this will be because, one, you're not marketing your business well, or two, your work needs improvement.

I admit that marketing in the wedding and event industry can be a tough nut to crack. There's a ton of different ways to market your business, and one marketing plan may work for one business and yet not for another. Regardless, marketing should be at the top of your to-do list. In fact, you should be reinvesting approximately 10% of your profits back into marketing dollars. Finding a marketing plan that works for you involves trial and error, but it's a perfect time when business is slow to try something new to help you get out of the rut.

If your work needs improvement, keep up the continuing education to master your craft, whatever it is in the event industry. Homing in on your specific skills must be an on-going effort, and this demands commitment. Technology keeps changing, and it will force you to adapt or die, but your craft in weddings and events is also an art form that requires constant reevaluation and reflection to continue improving.

If you're not getting new work, it may be because your craftwork simply isn't up to par by consumer standards, at least in terms of what constitutes professional services-grade work that is worth paying for. Be brave enough to ask your friends, clients and colleagues a simple question: "How can my work be improved?" The feedback may be painful to hear, but you and your business skills will grow because of it.

Warning Sign – 02

You Don't Have a Life

———————————

I can imagine that you didn't get into the wedding event industry to work non-stop, miss your son's soccer games and never spend time with your spouse or see your mother. During certain times of the year, that may sound like your life, but if this is your way of life consistently, it's most certainly time for a change. You should be running your business and not letting your business run you.

The first thing you probably need to do is outsource some of your work. This may mean hiring a post-production service for graphic design or social media or taking on an intern to help around with the office work. I know what you're thinking, "I can't afford to do that." But that's a lie and a cop-out. You can afford it. Figure out what outsourcing something will cost per job and then raise your prices by that much. If outsourcing your social media will cost you roughly $5,000 per year, and you do 20 events per year, then raise all your packages by $250. It's not even that significant a price increase, but you'll see a huge increase in the quality of your life. And that is worth much more than $250.

Can't figure out what to outsource? You should outsource things that fall into one of three categories:

1. Outsource what you hate doing. You don't build your dream business to spend your days toiling away at things you wish you weren't doing. Don't do them. Delegate them.
2. Outsource what you're not good at. Sometimes there are things that we absolutely love to do, but we just aren't that great at, or other people are better at them. Give your clients the best possible service and product by finding the best person for each job, even if it isn't you.
3. Outsource what slows you down. In the same way, there are things that you're not good at, and there are things that take you entirely too long to do. Your time as a business owner is valuable, spend it wisely and outsource the rest.

Warning Sign - 03

You Hate What You Do

This one is a biggie because it can be pretty damaging to the quality of your work as well as your life. You should never, ever hate what you do in life. That being said, maybe it's the end of wedding season and you're not making enough money, or you're constantly dealing with difficult clients.

Your feelings about what you do can result from any number of variables, but if the feeling has been sticking around for quite some time (I would say more than four months), then you need to figure out why you hate it. It's no use stomping your feet in an "I don't wanna" temper tantrum. That's just a waste of your time. Instead, identify what you hate to do and use that to start a list of things you need to change.

If your list of reasons why you hate being a business owner or visual artist becomes longer than the Great Wall of China, this may be an indicator that you are ready for a career change. More on that later. But for now, instead of focusing on that long list of "I hate" items, write a list of "I love" items, naming the things you do like about your current profession.

Warning Sign - 04

Your Clients are Angry With You

Difficult clients come by here and again, but if you're finding that your clients are upset more than 10% of the time, it's time to take a step back and look at what you may be doing wrong. Why are your clients upset most of the time? Are these things you can change?

For example, if your clients are upset with the turn-around time of your products, what can you do to speed that up? Perhaps they're not happy with the products you're providing them. It may be time to research a new fulfillment lab or album company.

Your clients and what they have to say about you will directly affect your quality of life (assuming you're stressed out by your clients being upset), your success in getting new business in the door and of course your overall income. Not sure what needs to change in order to get your clients from upset or okay to absolutely ecstatic about you? Try conducting an anonymous survey through Survey Monkey and ask them what you could do to better their customer experience.

Warning Sign - 05

You Can't Pay Your Bills

Whether you're in business to make a serious profit or just stay afloat, you have bills to pay. You have bills to put food on your table, and bills to buy new equipment.

If you're not paying your bills, or you're just making enough to scrape by and you're stressed out about not being able to scrape by next month, then you've got a significant problem. Luckily, this problem can be solved with simple math. Well, math and a little confidence. The solution is very straightforward: raise your prices.

Maybe you need to go back to the drawing board to reconstruct your pricing using the 1/3 Cost of Sales rule or making sure you have a "pull-through" into your high packages. Or perhaps you just need to be confident to know that your work is worth raising your prices to make ends meet. A great way to do this is to ask some colleagues in your area who have your same target market to review your packages and pricing and make suggestions that can help both you and your business succeed and thrive.

What if I have more than one warning sign?

If more than one of these warning signs resonates with you and your business, then you'll know that a big change is needed to get you, your business and your life back on track. If more than two of these resonated with you, take a look at what those are, as it may indicate a very big change is needed. For example, if you can legitimately say, "I'm not getting any new work, my clients are pissed at me, and I hate what I do," then maybe it's time to consider a complete career change. There's simply no need to be unhappy in life, and it's to no one's benefit for you to stay that way.

Regardless of whether you're weighing a big or small change, you'll need to muster up the courage to take the first step. I find there are three ways of mustering up courage: Meditation, Sharing and Support. Take time to meditate on and pray about your changes. Think about what you want to change and how you'll make it happen. Then, share your plans with those closest to you, such as family, friends and industry peers. Sharing your plans aloud makes them feel more real to you, and this will motivate you to follow through since you'll be accountable for what you've said. Finally, look for and ask for support from those same people. Ask them to follow up with you on your changes and encourage you along the way. A strong support system is a key motivator and will muster up the courage you wouldn't have otherwise.

Organizing for Efficiency

5 Apps to Save You Time and Organize Your Life

Work-life balance and managing your time are elemental in running a business. They are, in fact, aspects to master so that you can do more of what you became a business owner to do, shoot. Time-management can become very overwhelming as life continually throws new tasks at us. We must attend to the basic tasks of keeping our business sustainable. Social media requires our attention. And we must spend time cultivating relationships with our clients and potential clients. Finding shortcuts are crucial to managing it all. Below are five apps that I personally use and that I'm sure you will find useful.

▌ Every Post

Every time I see a new social media site, I simply want to jump off the bridge (but don't have the time to drive to the nearest one!). There's another social media venue for me to keep up with?! As if Pinterest, Google+, Google Pages, Facebook, Facebook Pages, Twitter, and LinkedIn aren't enough. Who can keep up with all of them and still run a business? You can.

EveryPost is an app (and I'm waiting, longingly, for them to make a desktop version) that allows you to simultaneously post to all of your social media sites I mentioned above and more. Not only will you be able to post content everywhere with just a few clicks, but you can customize each post, as well keep Twitter to 140 characters, tag people on Facebook, add hashtags on Google+, and set different privacy settings for each. #ThankYouSweetBabyJesus

There are a ton of other options for this kind of service. Later, Meet Edgar, Hootsuite, etc. go with the one that works best for you and your budget, and which saves you the most time.

Mileage Tracking

This app is not a receipt tracking app like Expensify (I could do a whole article comparing all of those), but it tracks a very important tax deduction, our mileage.

As a business owner you can deduct the mileage driven for work-related trips, such as going to weddings/shoots, meeting clients and traveling to networking events. It's not easy to keep track of mileage, and, in fact, it's quite annoying. But QuickBooks makes it easier, especially if you're already using it for accounting.

This app will let you track your mileage in myriad ways, including saving favorite trips (like driving to your studio or airport), GPS tracking and manually inputting values. It generates reports for you to hand right over to your accountant at the end of the year. Find an app that works for you to track your mileage mindlessly. Your wallet will thank you during tax season for keeping track of your mileage accurately!

Text Expander

If you've ever heard me speak, you've most likely heard me rave about this app for both desktop and mobile. It's hands-down the number one time-saver in my studio for the mundane task of writing emails. It makes responding to inquiries, booking couples and handling new employees super-fast and simple.

Text Expander allows you to save email templates (called snippets) within its interface and assign abbreviations to them. The program runs in the background of your desktop so that when you'd like to use one of the snippets, all you have to do is type in the abbreviation you made for it, and PRESTO, the whole email pastes right in. For example, when I receive an inquiry that I'm available for, I type in "IA" for "Inquiry Available," and my typical inquiry response email shows up. If I receive an inquiry that I'm not available for, I type in "TOOBAD," and in goes my "I'm sorry I'm not available" response. If I don't hear back from an inquiring couple, I type in "FU" to follow up.

You can add other features like prompts for filling in blanks in your templates or going with the newly updated mobile version (and syncing your templates). Text Expander is free to demo, and then you can buy it after your demo expires, which is actually pretty fun since it summarizes how many hours you've saved by using the product. It adds up very quickly. Gain back your time—so grab the app now.

■ Things

I confess that I use my Inbox and Google calendar like task lists. To an extent, I think Google actually designed them to be easily used that way, but opening your inbox and having to sift through unread messages to find your client's email is not only overwhelming but an unproductive waste of time.

Things is an (optional) cloud-based app that will operate and sync via mobile and desktop to help you organize your never-ending to-do list. You can organize your tasks into groups, such as "Today, Next, and Someday," as well as schedule them for dates in advance. You can schedule long-term project tracking and set up a simple inbox for tasks that you quickly identify without categorizing. You can attribute tags, check off completed items and even send the task to your email if you'd still feel more comfortable tracking your to-dos that way.

Things is free to try for 30 days, but then it costs a few dollars for the mobile app and about $40 for the desktop version. It's a little pricey as far as apps go, but the peace of mind is priceless.

Card Star

There's nothing that'll set your day into upheaval like trying to find something in a pile of similar shaped things, especially in your purse (hey ladies — we all have messy purses!). It's so easy to get frustrated over the little things like lost club cards. We'll tear apart our house to find what we need leaving us with another mess to deal with later.

I'm a huge saver-type person, so I belong to every free coupon and savings-card club known to mankind. Would I like to save 10% at Staples? You bet. Sign me up! You'll give me coupons for buying my dog, Tico, treats? I'm there. Before I knew it, my key chain and wallet had more plastic in them than a recycling factory. Anytime I wanted to use one of my discount or club cards, it took a handbag-dumping to find it.

Card Star takes away every one of those pieces of plastic and lets you put them right where they belong: in the recycling bin. Now when I sign up for a new freebie club, I scan the barcode into Card Star and throw the card away before I'm even finished checking out with the cashier. No more plastic, just cold, hard, saved cash and a warm fuzzy feeling whenever I look in my clean (ok, cleaner) pocketbook.

I had a hard time narrowing down my favorite apps to just five, and truthfully they always change and new things are added. Make sure you're subscribed to my YouTube channel where I always have new videos with ideas for efficiency: www.youtube.com/vanessajoy.

Digital Desktop Explosion

Ever feel like your computer's desktop just had a bomb go off on it? Or maybe finding a file just isn't the easiest thing to do during your day. So much of what we do as business owners is sitting in front of the computer, and if it's in disarray, then it can affect our productivity, state-of-mind and creativity.

There's nothing that'll get you overwhelmed faster than coming into work and facing a messy environment. Many of us aren't shooting as much during the winter, so take the time you would've spent in the studio or on location shooting and allocate some of it toward organizing your digital workspace. You'll feel better, be more productive, and you'll be ready for the next year's workflow by following a few of these steps to clean the digital clutter.

Clean desk, clean desktop

I've come to notice that when my actual physical desk is clean, my digital desktop soon follows. Messy habits are simply messy habits, and they have the same outcome whether in the tangible world or the digital one.

One of the first things you can do to start cleaning up your digital life is to start cleaning up your physical one as well. This might mean that every morning before you start work, you spend five minutes just straightening your desk, or you might do it during the last five minutes before you call it quits in the evening. Developing small, good habits like this one can have a compound effect on your life as a whole, and it will most certainly help teach you to organize your business on the digital front as well.

Once you have your organizational system worked out physically, you'll ideally transfer the same method to cleaning your desktop. After all, your desktop has all the same things like papers (files) and folders. You can even create an Inbox folder on your desktop if you'd like to throw everything without a home there until you can address it. Sometimes, just doing a clean sweep like making an Inbox pile can really help. Just be sure to get to it one day!

Saving to Desktop

I'm guilty of this one! I like to take quick screenshots that end up on my digital desktop and that stay there indefinitely. Or, if I don't know where to put a file, I'll leave it on my desktop. It's just like, if I don't know what to do with a piece of paper, I'll simply throw it anywhere on my desk. This habit (on both sides of the computer screen) leads to a messy work area that directly contributes to unproductively. Think about it: if your desk or desktop is full of papers or files, it'll take you longer to find the one you're looking for.

Not to fret. If you're like me and enjoy using your desktop interactively, you can still create order in the chaos. Create folders on your desktop that you can easily slide your files into to organize them. Folders like "{Insert Business Name Here}," "Screen Shots," and "Inbox" on your desktop will give you a place to quickly throw those files, so they're not cluttering your desktop. They'll be easy to find when you need them.

Organizing Your Desktop

There's another level of organization that your computer's desktop can achieve that'll bring you from merely functioning to thriving on the digital front. Folders are great, but organized folders in pretty boxes with bows are even better.

If you're a Windows user, check out Fences (http://www.stardock.com/products/fences/). Fences allows you to create shaded areas to organize your desktop, double click the desktop to hide or show icons, define rules to organize your desktop icons and a whole bunch more. If you're a Mac User, check out Desktop Groups (https://itunes.apple.com/us/app/desktop-groups/id542912361?mt=12), which is essentially Fences for Mac computers.

If you don't want to splurge for a program that does this for you, think about using your graphic design skills instead and create a backdrop that gives you sections to place your files into. This won't give you the functionality that other programs do, but it'll give you peace of mind when you look at your nice, clean computer.

Organizing Your Folders

Now that you have climbed out of the clutter that once filled your desktop, it's time to reign in how you sort the massive number of files that business owners have. It can be daunting, but once you have a concrete system in place, you'll have no trouble keeping it going. You'll be able to find anything you're looking for.

For shoots, I like to organize my folders by date. For every job I work, the main folder is labeled with "Year, Month, Day, Client Name." For example, a typical folder name you'd see on my computer is "2021 01 04 Juliana Martinez and Domenic Rosini Wedding." Having their names and the job type also helps me quickly search for their folder in the search function as well.

Inside the folder I have three separate folders: Originals — where I keep the RAW files; Jpgs — where I keep the culled and edited jpg proofs; and Slideshow — where I keep the jpgs from the same day slideshow I do the night of the wedding. From there, as orders are placed and albums are created, I'll create separate folders for each of those things with names like Album Design, Proof Book, and Retouched Images.

Having your folders organized in a consistent manner not only helps you find what you're looking for quickly, but it will make it easy for team members (like studio assistants and interns) to find the same files without having to ask you where they are. This is a huge time-saver all around.

■ Keep Up With It

The worst thing you can do is spend the time creating a system and then not actually use it. On the other hand, the best thing you can do is create a system and spend just a few minutes a day keeping it going steadily. Those little habits that help you maintain a tidy digital workplace will pay off in spades when you don't have to initiate a major cleaning spree every few months because it's gotten out of order. You'll be happy you developed those habits!

Perfecting Your Workflow

"It's digital. You can't even tell."

I remember the switch from film to digital like it was yesterday. We had to convince our clients that shooting with digital cameras wasn't a quality dip. We'd have them look at wedding albums that had film and digital images in there and ask if they could pick out which was which. I recall being proud when they thought a digital image was a film one.

And look where we are now. I'm about to write an article about your workflow, and it's all going to be a digital process. If I wrote this 15 years ago, a computer wouldn't have even come into the equation.

But what does that mean for you? Has life gotten easier? Nope. It has gotten harder. You have more to do and more possible ways to do it (i.e. screw it up). Clients are more demanding than ever, and marketing is a constant effort. So how do you keep up and maintain your sanity too?

Clients Come First

The first thing you should think about is your client's experience. What does their journey look and feel like throughout their time with you? Are there parts of your relationship where there's dead air? Are they waiting too long for images or products?

It can be very easy to forget what your work looks like from the client's perspective when we're knee-deep in business tasks. Make sure that whatever workflow decisions you make have their experience in mind. Always communicate the process with them and send reminders (I do mine via 17 Hats) so that they know you have them in the forefront of your mind.

Prioritize Marketing

One of the biggest mistakes I see business owners make in their workflow is forgetting that marketing needs to be included. Sure we may complain about the constant demands of social media marketing, but be happy about it. You have a free, open forum to market your business indefinitely. Use it.

Think about how you share images with other vendors. At what point do you select photos for your blog and your Instagram, Pinterest and Facebook pages? Event business owners, especially, when (and how) do you try to communicate with the venue about sharing an album of images for their salesroom?

I use Instagram for a lot of communication with venues. It tends to be a lower barrier to entry in getting contact information. I'll send photos that night that I took for a same-day edit (see my checklist for that at www.breatheyourpassion.com/sde), and I will build a relationship from there. When the proofs are complete, I will make sure to pick all of the favorites at that point. We will submit the images to publications via Two Bright Lights. Whatever you decide to do, make sure marketing is a staple in your workflow, or you'll find business easily slipping away from you.

Streamline What You Do

As much as I'd like to think I can roll over, snap some pics and sign autographs all day, that's just not realistic. I recently saw a beautiful meme of a ballerina's feet. One foot was wildly beautiful, perfectly on-point in her pretty pink ballet slipper, and the other foot was in the same pointed position but without the ballet shoe. You could see broken toes, cut up toenails and bandages everywhere. At the bottom of the meme was the inscription, "Everyone wants the success, but they don't want the work." Amen, ballerina. Amen.

Just because you're going to live and breathe your work doesn't mean you can't be smart about the work you have to do. Here's a list of my three favorite digital tools that help me manage the tasks I personally have to do.

- **IFTTT** is an app that fulfills commands based on cause-and-effect scenarios. If I post on Instagram, it'll automatically post the photo (not the link) on Twitter. If it's going to rain today, it'll send a reminder to my phone to take my umbrella in the morning.

- **Captio** allows you to email yourself with one tap. It's perfect for people like me who use their Inbox as a task list.

- **Later**. Okay, I confess that I personally don't use this because I've hired a social media manager. But she uses this and loves it. It's primarily focused on Instagram (which is great because so am I), but it also posts to Facebook and Pinterest and such. The best part is that the articles these guys send to their mailing list are fantastic. I get so much education from them on social media trends and tips that I'm literally never going to leave them.

And here are my top three photo workflow tools as well:

- **Photo Mechanic** is the fastest culling and renaming tool ever. It flows effortlessly and makes it possible for me to quickly find my favorite photos on the night of a wedding for the same-day edit.

- **Blogstomp**. While I've gotten away from logo-ing my images for social media, I use this as part of my same-day edit display. Using a digital picture frame, I perfectly display logoed photos from the wedding day. Brand recognition all night long!

- **Fundy Design Suite**. I mentioned before that I don't do the initial design, but I do sit with my clients in the album sales session and completely finish their album design right in front of them. We make whatever changes they want, and it's done by the end of a two-hour sales session. Better than done, my clients have been tripling the size of their albums this year!

Hopefully, this helps put a little perspective into your digital workflow. It's taken a long time to go from film to mastering this, and I want it to take much less time for you. That is until everything is Virtual/Augmented Reality, and it all changes again!

Outsourcing

5 Ways to Take 5 Things off Your Plate

The biggest hindrance that I hear business owners say they have when it comes to improving their workflow is that they're too far behind. It seems faster for them to do everything themselves rather than implement new methods that'll completely take the work off their plates.

But what's faster, doing it yourself or having someone else do it for you? Sure there's a learning curve, which is why now is the perfect time to execute new methods of getting work done better and faster than you have in the past. Make the changes now while you're still sunbathing on the shore, so to speak, before the work comes in like a tidal wave, and you're fighting to keep your head above water.

The first step to taking five things off your plate is to sit down and actually think about your workflow. Most business owners don't take the time to do this until they're emotionally compromised by being so overwhelmed with work that they can't process or visualize what needs to be done to make their business run smoother. I'm going to give you five ways to think about this now while you can still hear yourself think, so you can determine what five things you can realistically and beneficially take off your plate this year.

01 - Figure Out What You Want to Spend Your Time Doing

One would think this would be a no-brainer. Most of us became business owners because we wanted to do this job. We wanted to be our own boss, set our own hours, not be micro-managed and do what we love. Why then do so many of us allow ourselves to be side-tracked from doing what we love?

Evaluating how you spend your time starts with sitting down and reflecting on the things you want to do in your business. Dare I say, for you, that might not be taking pictures 100% of the time. When I started my business, I loved taking pictures above all else. But in owning and operating my business, I discovered that I really enjoyed marketing and networking with other wedding vendors and colleagues just as much. It's okay to discover the things that you want to do in your business.

This list will help you prioritize the tasks you should spend your time doing throughout the workday. You will recognize how little or how much you're actually doing those things. And this brings us to point number two.

02 - Determine What You Don't Want to Spend Your Time Doing

The saddest thing I see business owners do is spending their time doing something they hate. What is the point of owning your own business if you work day-in and day-out at things you don't want to do? You may as well have stuck with your day job and trudged away at that 9-5.

Even if you're a control freak, like most creatives are, I imagine there are certain things that you're doing that others could do better or faster. There may be things you simply don't want to spend your day doing. Take the time to make a list of the things that stress you out when you do them. What do you procrastinate doing? Or what do you simply dread having to do?

While you're making this list, it is not uncommon to feel guilty about realizing the things that you don't want to spend your time doing in your business. I want to take the time to reassure you that it's okay if you realize you don't want to spend your day in front of the computer editing in Photoshop or Lightroom. It's also absolutely okay to admit that marketing and accounting make you cringe.

It's also 100% okay to determine that you want a business that runs itself without you, even if that means you're not the one taking pictures 100% of the time. This is your business and your life. Continually doing things that you hate doing will only lessen your quality of life. Your business should improve your lifestyle, not make it more stressful.

03 - What is Sitting on the Back Burner?

How are you doing on your quarterly or yearly goals? Are you on track, or have those goals sat firmly on the same piece of scrap paper you wrote them on like an annoying coffee stain on your favorite shirt that just won't budge?

Go ahead and find that long list of things you want to do this year or should be doing that just aren't getting done. Whether it's long-term or short-term projects, a lot of times these are things that need to be done to improve our businesses. By not doing them, for whatever reason, only hurts our business.

Oftentimes we think that these types of projects are sitting on the back burner because we're the only ones who can do them. And while that might be true to an extent, you can often get help with them by a hiring company, asking a family member, or delegating to an employee. Don't let crucial, business-improving tasks fail to be completed because you're not letting anyone else help you do them.

It will be much more detrimental to your business to ignore these responsibilities, rather than having them done to only 80% of your satisfaction. Even then, you can finish up the last 20% yourself. Still, the task will have been accomplished, taken off the back burner, and erased from your mind.

David Allen, in his book "Getting Things Done," says that simply having things on your mind, even if they're not at the front of your mind, can be a huge creative hindrance and hurt your business in many ways. Let's be sure that we're not subconsciously hurting our creativity and the backbone of her business.

04 - What aren't you good at?

When I first started photography, back in the days of film, business owners didn't have the same types of responsibilities that they do now in the world of digital photography. For weddings, we would take the pictures and then send them off to the lab to be processed and wait for them to come back a week or two later. Now that digital has arrived, for some reason business owners are expected to be their own labs and do their own post-processing. But this was never the norm before. It's no wonder that a lot of business owners, especially the more seasoned professionals, aren't very good at doing their own post-processing.

While you may have already realized that you don't want to spend your time in Photoshop or Lightroom in step two, you may actually like doing your own post-processing, but by doing so, it actually hurts your business because your just not good at it. There are plenty of business owners who are amazing at taking pictures but don't know what they're doing processing them afterward. There wasn't anything wrong with that 20 years ago, so why should there be anything wrong with that now?

Take the time to make a list of the things you aren't good at. It could be anything from marketing and accounting to album designing and post-processing. While you should make sure that you are good at the things that you are doing in your business, you don't have to be the best at every aspect of your business. Good CEOs realize where they fall short in talent, skills or time, and they hire people to take over in those areas. You are the CEO of your business. Learn from them, admit what you're not good at, and find people willing to do those things for you.

05 - What Can You Afford?

Now that you have four lists that have helped you determine what five things (or more) you can take off your plate, it's time to determine how you are going to take them off your plate. This answer isn't the same for everyone, as we are all at different stages of business ownership and financial capability. Realistically, however, most of us can afford a lot more than we think we can if we figure out the full benefits of taking things off our plate.

For example, if you hire an office assistant $10 an hour to run to Staples, ship out albums, write some handwritten thank you notes, and answer a few inquiries and emails, that might cost you roughly $50 a week. In the extra five hours of time you have a week, you could easily develop relationships with other vendors in your area that will lead to referrals and booked jobs. This will make you a heck of a lot more than $50. With that mindset, you are actually spending, or wasting, a lot more money by not hiring that office assistant and doing all that mundane work yourself.

The same concept goes for anything you can delegate to an employee or outsource to a company. Sometimes, it's just a matter of raising your prices by a measly $100 to cover the cost of starting to outsource your post-production, album designs, or whatever else it is that could cost you money to stop doing yourself. Take the plunge. Invest in your business and your quality of life by figuring out what you can afford to take off your plate.

After determining some things that you can take off your plate, you still want to have a workflow system in place that runs smoothly and efficiently. Check out this video that shows off one of my favorite new toys. It has helped me get one of my most frequent tasks done faster than I ever thought I could. I'll give you a hint. "Look, Mom! No hands!"

Preparing Mentally for Outsourcing

Kill your darlings, kill your darlings.

Kill your darlings, even when it breaks your egocentric little scribbler's heart, kill your darlings.

Stephen King

There comes a point in our businesses when we simply can't do it all ourselves. For me, that came about three years into my business. Even though I was already outsourcing my post-production work to Evolve Edits (now I'm with Shoot Dot Edit) and my house cleaning to Molly Maids, I still had too much to do and too little time to do it. I needed help to keep my customers happy and, more importantly, keep me happy and less stressed.

Even if you're a control freak, like most creatives are, there are certain things that you're doing that others could do better and faster or that you simply don't want to spend your day doing.

In this chapter, you're going to make a list of the things that stress you out when you do them, things you're not good at, things that you procrastinate doing, or simply things you dread having to do. It could be anything from marketing and accounting to album designing and post-processing. This list will be individual to you.

But this can get tricky mentally. You have to start thinking like a CEO by hiring, training and trusting vendors or employees. This will take time. Good communication and patience are key to any new hire. There is a learning curve on both sides. But stick to it, and you'll watch your business start flowing like a well-oiled machine.

It's important not to let ego get in the way. Oftentimes projects aren't being completed and clients are being let down because a business owner fails to delegate responsibility correctly. Don't let crucial, business-improving tasks fail to be completed because you're not allowing anyone else to help you do them. It will be much more detrimental to your business to ignore these responsibilities, rather than having them done to only 80% of your satisfaction.

Tim Ferris talks about the statistics of learning a language, and I think it relates to this pretty well. He says it takes only six months of everyday practicing to learn a language to about an 80% fluency. As someone who speaks three languages myself, 80% is pretty impressive. This level of fluency will enable you to speak a language to anyone at any time and communicate anything you need.

Do you want to know how long it takes to reach 96% fluency? 20 years. 20 years! The difference between 80% and 96% is minute, especially when coming from your perfectionist perspective versus your client's consumerist perspective. 80% satisfaction for you is likely 96% satisfaction for your client and a far better outcome than late deliveries and unfinished products.

While you should make sure you know how things operate in your business, you don't have to be the best in every aspect of it. Good CEOs realize where they fall short in talent, skills, and time, and they hire other people to take over in those areas. Your business gets better as you bring in the best people for each job. The quality of your business increases and your turnaround time becomes faster, resulting in a better product and happier clients.

You are the CEO of your business. Learn from others before you, admit what you need help with, and find the right companies or people to do those things for you. Let experts do expert work for your business rather than accept your own mediocre work.

While making this list, it is not uncommon to feel guilty about realizing the things you don't want to spend your time doing in your business. I want to take the time to reassure you that it's okay if you realize you don't want to spend your day in front of the computer editing in Photoshop or Lightroom. It's also absolutely okay to admit that marketing and accounting make you cringe. It's also 100% okay to determine that you want a business that runs itself without you, even if that means that you're not the one taking pictures 100% of the time. This is your business and your life, and if you continually do things you hate, it will only lessen your quality of life. Your business should improve your lifestyle, not make it more stressful.

When I first started photography back in the days of film, business owners didn't have the same responsibilities that they do now in the world of digital photography. For weddings, we would take the pictures, send them off to the lab to be processed, and then wait for them to come back a week or two later. Now that digital is here to stay, for some reason business owners are expected to be their own labs and do their own post-processing, and yet this was never the norm before. It's no wonder that a lot of business owners, especially more seasoned professionals, aren't very good at doing their own post-processing. With a genuine heart, I'm going to tell you that outsourcing your post-production is one of the biggest leaps toward getting your life back.

I have one final thought on outsourcing and why it's so crucial for creative business owners. David Allen, in his book "Getting Things Done," says that simply having things on your mind, even if they're not at the forefront of your mind, can be a huge creative hindrance and hurt your business in many ways. Let's be sure that we're not subconsciously hurting our creativity and the very backbone of our business.

What to Outsource

Not sure what you should outsource? Start with these five things.

Anything You Don't Like Doing

The saddest thing I see business owners do is spending time doing something they hate. What is the point of owning your own business if you work day-in and day-out at things you don't want to do? You may as well have stuck with your day job and trudged away at that 9-5.

Anything You're Not Good At

While you may have already realized that you don't want to spend your time in Photoshop or Lightroom in step two, you may actually like doing your own post-processing. But by doing so, it actually hurts your business because you're not great at it. There are plenty of business owners who are amazing at taking pictures but just don't know what they're doing processing them afterward. There wasn't anything wrong with that 20 years ago, so why should there be anything wrong with that now?

Anything That Slows You Down

Your turnaround time gets faster when you let someone else do things that slow down your day. That means happier clients and more business because you can concentrate your efforts on things that aren't hindering your workflow.

Anything That You Could Pay Someone Else Minimum Wage to Do

Things like mailing products, running to the office supply store or not having your bills on auto-pay are a sad waste of your time and talents. Find little things, one thing at a time, that won't take more than a few minutes to teach someone else, and let them go do it.

Anything That Would Enhance Your Client Experience

Walk through your client experience from start to finish. At what point in the relationships are they sitting around waiting for you? Where could you give them more personalized service? Perhaps it's time to start thinking about a receptionist or a phone, email and lead answering service like 17Hats Ally. In the fast-paced culture we live in today, it's often the early bird that gets the worm. Analyze where you can improve your customer service and experience and make it happen.

What Not To Outsource

On the other side of outsourcing is realizing that there are places you have to be and things you need to do yourself. Unless you're planning on creating a company that entirely runs without you (which would be fine but not quite the business type we're talking about in this book), you need to be present at specific times.

The upside of this is that when you're outsourcing, you're making time for these tasks that are most important for you to dedicate time to. You get to do the things you like doing in your business, such as taking pictures or meeting with clients. Your time will be spent on the crucial tasks that give you the biggest return on investment, such as networking with other vendors and building your photography and business knowledge. You'll spend time working on your business rather than in your business.

Let's put this to practice. Take a sheet of paper, and draw a line down the middle, creating two columns. On the left side, write a list of things you hate or aren't good at or things that slows you down. Pay someone else to do these tasks, thereby enhancing the client's experience.

On the right side, write the things you like to do and the things you are good at. Write down where clients need to see your face.

When you first start your business, this list may lean heavily to the right, with few items on the left. It's important to come back to this list periodically, especially when you're feeling overwhelmed with work, and update it.

Financially preparing for outsourcing

Now that we've covered the importance of outsourcing and its positive effect on your business, financially preparing is the easy part. It's all literally black and white because it's math.

Outsourcing will ultimately affect your cost of sales, which is part of how you build your pricing. You've already done the hard part in creating your pricing and packaging, so at this point, when you're adding costs by outsourcing, don't overthink it. If you're going to start having someone design your wedding albums, and it costs you $150 per album to do so, then raise all of your packages with albums in them by $150. Increase them more later, so you end up following the three-times cost of sales rule. But for now, begin by covering your costs to establish, support and fall in love with the new outsourcing routine.

I know what you're thinking. "I can raise my prices now, but I won't see that change happen until a year from now when I get paid for that wedding." This is true. But this doesn't mean that you wait to outsource until that first wedding rolls around when you've technically charged them for the outsourcing. That would be insane. This process means that you're making an initial investment into bettering your business. You do this when you buy equipment, rent studio space and purchase advertisements. Investing in your business before seeing the ROI (Return on Investment) is something you'll repeatedly do as a business owner.

I'm not telling you to go into debt to start outsourcing (or for any other business investment, for that matter). You can start by saving a chunk of money ahead of time to cover upcoming outsourcing costs. Alternatively, you can pull back from other investments (like that new lens I know you want) to give into one that'll improve your overall business.

While we're on the subject of buying equipment versus investing in outsourcing, I have to say this. As a photographer, I love camera gear, and at this point, because I've run my business correctly, I own almost every bit of gear I want to own. However, if you're in the season of your business where cash flow is tight, and you have to decide whether to buy that new lens or invest in outsourcing, you need to ask yourself one question. "Which investment will my clients notice more?" In other words, which investment will directly affect them more: you outsourcing so that their products are better and delivered to them sooner or you having a new piece of equipment where only you and your business owner friends see the difference? First, choose what affects your clients the most, and then invest in the rest.

When you're getting ready to outsource parts of your workflow, you'll have to do fairly extensive research to find the companies (or staff, but more on that later) that will be best for you. This is where trade shows come in. Industry conferences and conventions are great for networking, learning and definitely partying, but they're also the best place to be when you're looking for new vendors.

When I first started offering albums to my clients, I didn't do my research online. I went to countless trade shows and inspected each album to look for flaws like bad binding, pinking in the seam, warping in the pages, etc. After I narrowed them down by their product, I met the employees and sometimes the owners of the different companies to see how they operate. If I can give you any advice at all on choosing vendors, it would be to choose ones that know what customer service is all about. Every company will make a mistake here and there, but it's more important that they know how to solve them quickly and to your satisfaction.

During this time I dealt with an album company that will remain nameless because I do hope they've changed their ways at this point. I loved their product. It was perfect, unique. My clients were head-over-heels for their albums. So, I ordered my first client album from them. It was a 10"x10," 20-page, flush-mounted album. When it came in the mail, I thought it looked a little small. I measured it, and it was actually a 9"x9" album. I figured there was some kind of mistake and contacted the company. The owner himself called me and tried to tell me that somewhere on the website it says that 10"x10"s are really 9"x9"s. For the record, I looked all over the website and couldn't find this, but that is not the point. The point is that I was a first-time customer, and instead of keeping me for life by making this right, even though he thought it was my mistake by not finding the fine print, his actions and belittling words toward me made sure that I never used their product again (and none of my friends, colleagues or mentees did either).

I have positive experiences of customer service, too, such as my experience with another album company, which I will name, PictoBooks. PictoBooks is one of the very first flush-mount album manufacturers in the United States. They have a superior product line with incredibly gorgeous cover choices. Like I mentioned before, everyone makes mistakes, and Picto made one with one of my orders.

When I brought a printing error to their attention, not only did they immediately replace the books, but they changed their entire printing process to improve production for my future orders and all of their existing customers as well. That is what excellent customer service is all about. Look for that in your vendors. In fact, be that in your business. Be Picto.

Hiring and training staff

If you're already managing staff, whether independent contractors, interns or employees, you know what a difficult task it can be. It's not easy to find the right person for the job. When you finally do find them, the training process that happens afterward can be even harder and in some ways more work.

There are many common pitfalls you can avoid with your staff if you choose to hire individuals. Problems like high turnover, excessive training time, over-paying and micro-managing can be damaging and expensive to you and your staff. We'll discuss the basic steps to hiring and training staff in this chapter that will teach you not only how to prevent those issues but to enjoy the people you have working for you.

Know your demographic

This is a concept that we normally apply to our customers. Are you a wedding business owner? Then your target demographic is normally women between 22 and 28. Senior portrait business owner? You're looking for teenagers from 15 to 17 years old. When it comes time to hire someone, you also need to know the demographic of the person that will typically fit the bill. The easiest way to find this out is by figuring out how much you can pay the employee and what type of person can live off that wage.

If you're looking to hire an intern that you're paying with experience rather than in cold hard cash, you're most likely not going to have luck bringing on a person who lives on their own and has a lot of bills to pay. This is why typically college-age students work well as interns, particularly if they're getting college credit for it. If you are looking to hire someone for pay, they need to be in a position where the money you're offering can sustain them. If you can only pay $20,000 per year, a person supporting a family of 5 most likely isn't going to be what you're looking for.

Of course, this is not to discriminate against anyone, but it's to help give more clear direction toward making both the employee and employer happy in the job. Hiring someone outside the job demographic may result in a higher turnover rate because the salary isn't enough to sustain their lifestyle. A high turnover rate will cost your business money and time having to train new people more frequently. It also may result in you paying an already trained staff member more than the job is worth because you can't lose them and then afford to spend the time training someone new. Overpaying is not a place you want to be either.

Furthermore, knowing your demographic will help you anticipate turnover with your current employees. You can be prepared for it. If you've had someone working for you for a few years and they're beginning to outgrow the demographic of the job, it's probably time to start finding and training their replacement. Ideally, the staff member who is leaving will train the staff member who is onboarding. This way, you don't have to dedicate your time to training, and you're essentially outsourcing that as well.

■ Have a relevant interview process

I remember an old job I had in a marketing department of a large franchise organization that was looking to hire a new marketing assistant. One of the higher-ups was pulling together questions to ask the applicants, and I'll never forget one of them. "If you were a car, what kind and color would you be?"

Really? Unless the marketing position was in a car dealership, I, to this day, find these types of questions useless in determining if an applicant is fit for a cubicle desk job in marketing. Sure, there's most likely some psycho-analysis reason for that question, such as determining personality and probable work ethic. But that's not going to tell me if that person can produce the kind of work I'm looking for. If I ever had to answer that question, I'd likely be labeled as unhireable. I'd have literally no answer because I couldn't care less about something as ridiculous as a personified car metaphor. We'll leave that to Disney.

In my opinion, there's only one way to find out if an applicant can produce the kind of work you're looking for. They have to demonstrate their ability to do the job you want them to do.

A few years back, when my husband Rob Adams was looking to hire a new film editor for his cinematography company www.robadamsfilms.com, we had a two-step interview process. First, we'd have applicants send us their portfolio of editing work. If it passed our expectations at that point, we sent them a short film to edit. Nothing crazy and only a 45-60 second video, so it wasn't taking up too much of their time. It also wasn't real work that needed to get done. That would be unethical, in my opinion, and could become a problem if you assigned a time-sensitive task to an interviewee that never got completed. This interviewing method made it possible for us to see how they would do the exact work we needed them to do. From there, we were better able to make an informed decision.

When I hire new second shooters, I have a similar process. First, I talk with them via video chat or in person to see if they have basic professionalism and to give them an idea of what the job entails. If they pass my first-round interview, I ask them to come along and third shoot a wedding with me. This acts as the last part of the interview process and, in reality, the first part of the training process as well. I can see how they perform at a wedding in the same conditions and circumstances I'm in, alongside them. I can see their behavior and mannerisms and, most importantly, how they present themselves in front of clients. All things their favorite car and color could never tell me.

Ultimately, I would advise you to hire for character over skill every time. You can teach skills. But character traits have already been developed and are hard to create or break. Every now and then, I have a candidate come up that doesn't have all the skills needed for the job, but passes with flying colors in demonstrated work ethic, professionalism and initiative. You don't want to let go of these kinds of people just because their skill level isn't up to par yet. Hold onto them and train them, granted not on your dollar, and see if you can build them up into a roll you need. If they're financially able to swing it, they'll be forever grateful to the person who first believed in them, and you'll be rewarded with a loyal employee and colleague.

Create a Job Description

This step is easily skipped over. Business owners usually don't fit into or keep a strict job description because, while we're labeled business owners, our job description really entails so much more. However, we can't expect our employees to work the same kind of crazy hours and multiple job positions within our business as we do. In the same way that we manage client expectations to keep them happy, we need to manage our staff expectations as well.

Creating a job description will help you in your search. It will force you to define what it is that you're looking for. This seems simple, but so many people skip this step, not realizing the effects it has. Without a job description, you may as well be grasping in the dark, trying to find a puzzle piece when you have no idea of the shape you're looking for.

The first step to creating a job description for the person you're looking to hire is to create your job description. Itemize and list all of the things you're required to do in your business and maybe even separate them into sections depending on the task (i.e. a marketing and advertising section, an office reception section, etc.). Then, take a look at the things you don't want to do and that you're looking to have your staff take over. From that point, you can start building a job description for your staff member.

Having a job description will be beneficial for both you and your staff. It helps guide the interview process, so you have a clearer idea of the person you need to hire. Once you hire them, it defines their role in your company, which gives them clear goals and knowledge of what's expected of them. Finally, it helps keep you in check to make sure you're not giving them unfair tasks that are outside their job description. Duties that they're not expecting could consequently anger your staff and leave them feeling like they're being taken advantage of.

What Kind of Staff Member?

Determining the kind of staff member you need is a critical part of hiring and managing your staff, and one that entails some legalities as well. Are you looking for an employee or independent contractor, and what are the rules for each?

Normally, photography businesses hire independent contractors because you don't have to pay payroll tax for them as you do for employees. You also don't fall under and a plethora of laws and requirements involved for employees, such as mandatory healthcare options and the like. At the end of the year, you hand independent contractors a 1099 telling them what they made that year and that's it. You aren't responsible for taking out their income taxes or anything else. It's the easier of the two to manage, but the government can come down on companies and fault them, saying that their independent contractors are really employees, which will result in some hefty fines.

How do you determine whether your staff is legally an employee or an independent contractor? There are a lot of gray areas here because work situations can vary so much. Some of the big questions to ask are, "Does the staff member work for other companies as well?", "Does the staff member submit an invoice for payment?" and "Are they paid per hour or per gig?"

It can be confusing, so be sure to check with the stipulations on the IRS website to get your information straight from the source. Here's a link to the IRS page that will help you better understand the two roles: http://www.irs.gov/Businesses/Small-Businesses-&-Self-Employed/Independent-Contractor-(Self-Employed)-or-Employee%3F.

Be sure to have a contract with your staff member clearly stating that they are one or the other. The contract should also affirm that the IRS's stipulations are the determining factors in categorizing an employee or independent contractor. For example, an independent contractor's contract should state that they are using their own equipment and taking on their own expenses to complete the job, just to name a couple stipulations.

Regardless of which kind of employee you decide is best for you to have on staff, how you address them is a completely different story. Many business leadership gurus will tell you to address them as team members. "Staff" and "employees" imply that they're hired help and not a part of the bigger picture. When people that work for you don't feel like a part of the team, they don't have the same motivation toward their jobs. When they are team members, and you give them the whole picture, they can see what they're working toward and understand how they are a part of it.

I can attest to the truth of titles by remembering when I was a second shooter for the wedding business owner I first worked for. When we would walk into the bride's house, I was always introduced as his assistant. The first year or so while I was learning the ropes, that was fine. As I advanced in the company and took on more responsibilities in marketing and sales, I grew to hate being referred to as just the assistant. I brought it up to him, and he started introducing me as his associate. I was overjoyed. It's amazing how changing four little letters motivated me to do more and be more in the company. Everyone benefits.

Training New Staff

The goal of training your new staff members is to be efficient and effective, maximizing and managing their time with tools you can use to make your lives easier. While training new staff will take time, it doesn't have to throw a wrench in your production schedule.

Train Them Right

Training staff doesn't have to be difficult or an overwhelming task. It does take time to do, but it doesn't have to be time wasted. The first thing to remember is that your staff member is not you. It'd be nice if we could clone ourselves, but we can't, and we can't expect our staff to morph into our clone or read our thoughts, for that matter. Training will take both communication and time.

The key to training staff is to train them strategically so that their skills build upon each other. The first thing I teach my office assistant or intern when they start is how to work my album building program, Fundy Album Builder. I do this because I'm teaching them a skill that they'll use to complete multiple projects in the office. Next, I'll teach them our shipping system. Again, this is a skill that I can have them use on more than one occasion.

Understandably, we're business owners with photography training, not teachers with educational training, so teaching someone the ropes doesn't necessarily come naturally to us. Having a Bachelor's degree in Education, I learned a simple, four-step method to teaching effectively during one of my college education classes. Since then, I've used the same process to teach my staff and many business owners around the world.

1. Tell. Explain the content in detail.
2. Show. Demonstrate the task you want to teach.
3. Walk Through. Guide them through the same task, allowing them to do it themselves while you watch. Help as needed.
4. Observe. Watch while they do the task on their own, but this time, don't correct them when they make mistakes. Let them work through the process until the end before correcting mistakes. Ideally, they'll start to recognize the mistakes on their own. You may need to repeat this step a few times.

■ Pass It On

Let them teach the skill to someone else. Being able to teach a skill to someone else indicates mastery of that skill.

To bring it all home, you need to teach them why you do what you do instead of just how you do it. This helps them make good decisions on their own without having to nag you for every little thing. Dave Ramsey teaches this concept in his book EntreLeadership and says, "Guiding values make decisions clearer. "

Ramsey suggests that teaching them to understand your thinking methods is more important than anything else. When they have a problem, instead of them coming to ask for the solution to that problem, ask them to come up with three or more possible solutions, plus their suggested course of action. Have them bring those solutions to you and then discuss which you would pick and why. After doing this a few times, your staff member should start to see a pattern and be able to determine what it is that you want without needing to constantly interrupt you for input.

This will also empower them in their position and make them feel trusted and credible in the company. You can continue to give them freedoms like this and put your money where your mouth is. Tim Ferris, in his book The Four Hour

Workweek, advises that you permit certain staff members to make monetary decisions on their own up to a $100 value (or whatever value you'd like to attribute). I have personally found this very freeing in my business and have even gone as far as to give one of my staff members a business credit card. My office manager doesn't need to come to me and ask if she can order more envelopes or anything else needed for the office. I give her the freedom just to do what needs to be done and tell me about it later.

Create a List of Responsibilities

I first learned to create task lists while I was working as a Marketing Associate for Lawn Doctor, a 350+ franchise company based in New Jersey. Task lists help both you and your staff member keep track of responsibilities and workload. A list of responsibilities will help maximize your staff's efficiency and manage their task's priorities.

Their task list should first be created by you and derived from the job description you created for them earlier. The task list should be divided into short term, long term and on-going projects to ensure that your staff always knows what they should be doing. If things are slow in the short-term tasks, they have long term projects to work on.

Use Tools to Assign Tasks Easily

Giving your staff members new tasks shouldn't be a chore or take too much time to accomplish. There are many different methods to maintain clear communication with new or ongoing tasks. Evernote or Google Documents are live documents that allow you to maintain a task list that both you and your staff can access and change. Personally, I use my email as a task list for myself, so when new tasks (i.e. emails from clients asking for things) come in, I simply forward the emails to the staff that I want to assign the task to. Use whatever works best for you: white boards, planners, post-it notes. Just be sure it's both consistent and clear.

Thankfully, many client management systems have developed a task-based workflow system within their software. 17Hats, which I'm currently using, assigns a workflow to each project based on what the project is. It'll give you timed or process-determined tasks like "email to schedule engagement session" or "create wedding album design" that you can check off as they're completed. This may not seem important when you only have one or two clients in the beginning, but it will be crucial as your business grows. I can't stress enough how important it is to build the correct foundation for your business so that it grows concretely over the years. 17Hats is a great system to start with because you can use it for free up to a limited amount of clients.

Anticipate Turnover

As we discussed, the job position you're offering will most likely cater to a certain demographic depending on workload, salary and lifestyle. Eventually, even your best staff member will grow out of the demographic and need to move on. It's just the life cycle of your job position, but it doesn't have to throw you for a loop.

Knowing your demographic will help you anticipate turnover with your current employees and be prepared for it. If you've had someone working for you for a few years and they're beginning to outgrow the demographic of the job, it's probably time to start finding and training their replacement.

If you don't, you run the risk of overpaying the existing staff member simply because you weren't prepared for turnover and you need them to stay until you are. It's just not a good position to be in for you or the staff member. If you have a staff member who is ready to move on, no amount of money will make them happy staying where they don't want to be.

Avoid waiting until the last minute to train your replacement. This will leave you in a rut, likely to hire an unsuitable replacement for time's sake and leave you to retrain the new staff member from scratch. Ideally, the only time you should have to train a new staff member from scratch is the first time you hire a staff member for that position. After that, your senior staff member should participate in training his or her replacement or a new colleague. Not only will this lessen the stress and time commitment on your part, but it also gives your new staff member multiple teachers to help them train. It will add to the trust you give your existing staff member and promote a team-centered work environment. You should still supervise and participate in the new staff member's training, just allow the bulk of the task training to be done by the senior staff member.

■ What to Pay

Appropriate compensation will vary depending on where you live in the country and what you can afford, given your business' income level. One of the best things you can do to discover what you should pay is research. Ask other professionals in your area, preferably ones that you already have a relationship with, what they think is fair or what they're paying their staff members with a similar job description. You can also ask for advice from local photography groups like Better Together Facebook Groups, PPA Local Chapters and the like. This will prevent you from over- or underpaying your staff, and it will prepare you for determining your cost of sales on any given job. Also, consider asking how they pay their staff members (per diem, salary or hourly), taking into consideration their legal staff position (employee or independent contractor).

Keep in mind that you can also use pay as an incentive for exceptional performance. Creating a bonus system to motivate staff members can be rewarding for everyone involved. Keep the bonuses (or penalizations) consistent with staff performance and fair to the task and all involved, and you'll have success. I've also experimented with offering a commission on sales for my office manager, who does most of the communicating with my couples throughout our relationship with them. So far, both systems have worked very well.

Ultimately, no matter how you end up paying your staff, you want to make sure they feel appreciated past monetary compensation. Getting paid well is one thing, but making them feel valued is priceless. Take the extra time and effort to make your staff feel appreciated. It will mean a lot more to them than making one more dollar an hour above the area average. You can do this in many different ways, such as writing encouraging notes, buying (or making) them lunch every once in a while, or getting them a thank-you gift every now and again. Be creative and genuine, and you can't go wrong.

■ What if?

This is one of the biggest fears I hear from business owners looking to hire help. What if their new hire leaves and starts their own business? What if I invest in them, teach them all of my secrets and then they become my competition? Nobody likes the idea of training the competition.

This is a culture, and particularly an industry, where everyone believes they are destined to own their own business and be their own boss. It can be frustrating working with employees and contractors with that mindset because you may fear them taking your hard-earned knowledge to their business. Guess what? It will happen. There is a better solution than fearing the inevitable and being bitter about it. Instead, be supportive, just as someone was once supportive of you. Be humble and not better than them, and later, maybe they'll end up being the ones that help you.

I would suggest bringing people slowly into the inner workings of your business. For example, if you hire an office manager, start off with the day-to-day tasks like shipping products and dealing with ordering and incoming mail. If they prove their worth and that they're not just around to suck up all they can and then leave, you can expand your training. Move on to showing them more of what you do for marketing. Let them handle some of your trade secrets if it's appropriate to lighten your workload.

If you ever decide you want to show them the financials of the business, avoid a key mistake I've seen firsthand. Do not show them your income without giving them a clear understanding of your expenses. A colleague of mine recently made this mistake, and it resulted in a greedy employee. That employee kept wanting more and more money because, from her perspective, without seeing the costs of running the business, he was raking it in.

My office manager sees what comes in, but she also sees what goes out. I have her place orders, run payroll and even write out my hefty quarterly tax payments. As a result, she has a better understanding of the profit and loss of my company, and therefore she doesn't feel the resentment that would naturally come with a skewed perspective of seeing only the income.

▮ Get Started!

It's one of life's great oxymoron's that we can find a multitude of ways to make our lives better and more efficient, including when we hire people, and yet still end the day wishing there were a few more hours in it. As human beings, I think we have the tendency to find ways to do things faster only to fill that newly found time with more to-do's and deadlines. While this chapter aims to give you ways to make your life easier and save you time, I also want to challenge you to fill that saved time intentionally. Dare I say, don't fill it with work, but fill it with life!

▮ Chapter Checklist

- ☑ Mentally prepare for outsourcing
- ☑ Create a list of things to outsource
- ☑ Create a list of things you shouldn't outsource
- ☑ Research vendors using a vendor worksheet
- ☑ Adjust pricing to accommodate for the raised cost of sales
- ☑ Decide if hiring in-studio is right for you
- ☑ Begin the hiring process with relevant interviewing
- ☑ Complete team member training with patience, communication and the 4-Step Teaching Method
- ☑ Always anticipate turnover

Wowing Your Clients

In this article you'll learn how to:

- Do less work after a wedding
- Do more marketing that takes less time
- How to make your clients go gaga over you

"How did you DO this?!"

I remember watching her exclaim with her jaw on the floor shortly before turning to her bridesmaid standing next to her, saying, "Can you believe this?!" She was holding her wedding pictures in her hand before the wedding had even finished. I was her hero, even if for just that moment.

You've probably heard the term "same-day edit" before. Typically, it refers to wedding business owners presenting a slide show of images from the wedding day during the reception. It is that, but it can be so much more.

The first time I printed a mini-album for my couple during their wedding, I did it all alone. I had no assistant, just an extra business owner to take my place while I worked. Since then, I've realized I'm more valuable behind the camera than behind the computer, and now my assistant does most of the work. Thanks to this process, I've been able to get done the night of the wedding what most business owners spend doing all the following week.

Here's what I do the night of the wedding:

- A slideshow, presented at the reception;
- A same-day album, given at the reception;
- Photos uploaded and tagged on Facebook;
- A favorite photo posted and hashtagged on Instagram;
- A client SmugMug Gallery;
- An Animoto Slideshow;
- A blog post that is 95% finished; and
- Photos ready for submission to blogs and magazines

It's a ton of stuff, but it's not impossible. In fact, it's almost easy. During the reception, what do you have your assistant doing anyway? I taught a full-day course on the how-tos of getting the most done at a wedding. You can see it on creativeLIVE. Or you can check out this video for the crash course: https://www.youtube.com/watch?v=o7CENda5L8k.

Now I know that this is photographer-specific, but you can find ways to surprise your clients no matter what you do. A little something thoughtful goes a long way and gives you clients something to talk about.

VANESSA JOY
EDUCATION

3 Keys to High-end Weddings

One of the goals on a lot of wedding business owner's vision boards is the high-end wedding. Depending on where you are in the world, this can have a very different connotation. I'm in the New Jersey and New York City area, one of the most expensive places to have a wedding, so high-end to me means multi-million-dollar weddings at places like Cipriani and The Plaza. High-end to others might just mean you want to consistently work at the best wedding venue places in town.

Whichever it is for you, it most certainly means that you have to find and appeal to a more luxurious client. This isn't easy, especially if you don't run in those crowds yourself (heck—I sure don't). But there are ways to position yourself and your brand so that you can get in front of those clients and make them beaming-happy when you do.

Client Experience

This is, above all, the most important part of photographing a high-end wedding. I know, you expected me to start with "here's where you get high-end leads." Guess what? There's no magic to that other than targeting your marketing and advertising toward them (which is another article in itself).

The problem that most business owners face is not knowing how to give those prospects an experience that makes the pickiest of couples begging for more.

To top it off, word-of-mouth is touted to be one of the best forms of marketing. Well, if you want your couples talking about you, then give them something to talk about! This is true regardless of where your ideal client falls on the low- to high-end wedding spectrum. It's even more so true if you're aiming high. High-end couples expect a superior experience from you just as they expect a superior experience from where they bought their Porsche.

Here are some ways you can ensure you're giving a stellar experience to everyone who walks through your door.

Give, give, give, and then give some more. Give gifts and surprises they don't expect. Don't give discounts (that's very anti-high-end), but give gifts in your photography packages if you'd like.

Over-compensate if something goes wrong. Things go wrong, but if you give them way more than is required to make it right, you're going to end up on top.

If you meet them in person, act like their patrons at your high-end restaurant. Give them food, wine, hang up their coats, and set the ambiance—everything you'd expect when walking into a Michelin-star restaurant.

Ask what they need. Always keep the lines of communication open and be one step ahead of them. It's better to set yourself up to answer questions before they ask them and get them to open up with whatever they'd like from you before they feel the need to ask for it.

■ Appearance

Don't think I'm telling you to go out and buy a $1,000 suit. I'm not. However, there's a lot to be said to being relatable to your client. Since your client only knows you skin-deep, the superficial is all they have to start with in finding a connection with you—at least for now.

If you can't afford to buy some kind of statement piece that'll bring up your relatability to high-end clients (and again, I'm not saying to go into debt or buy something you can't afford), then educate yourself on them. It's a trivial example, but if you don't know why those red soles are important on a bride's wedding shoes, then there's a chance they're not going to look at you like you understand what's important throughout the day.

I remember the first time I second shot for a high-end wedding business owner in NYC. I literally did not understand most of the words that were coming out of the bride and wedding planner's mouths, and I'm pretty sure I embarrassed myself with the clothes I chose to wear as well. Now, I'm glad for experiences like those, and if you get a chance, do second shoot for other business owner's high-end weddings, if at all possible.

There are a lot of other ways to brand your appearance and business. So, if you want a little homework, grab my free eBook, 9 Secret Ways to Brand Your Business, at bit.ly/joybrand.

Social Media Presence

Most of what I told you above comes into play once you have clients contacting you and you get a chance to meet or work with them. This tip comes before that, and, therefore, it is actually more important than the first two because it's your initial impression. Facebook, Pinterest and Instagram are 110% your storefront, even more than your website at times.

If you don't have those three social media accounts, now is the time to go and get them. Prospective clients look at your social presence and judge your credibility and capability from them. It's sad, but it's true. Here are three ways that you can make sure that you're putting your best foot forward online.

1. Post often—at least once a day.
2. Engage others by liking, commenting and sharing other posts.
3. Have consistent visuals and voice. Instagram, in particular, is your new portfolio.

Even if you're not looking to tap into the high-end market, all of these concepts apply. As the world becomes smaller and consumers grow further educated on how solid brands and businesses operate, the more expectant they'll be of what they experience with you. Give yourself a leg up and start reflecting on what your business speaks to clients. Make positive changes along the way. You and your clients will be happy you did!

Boosting Your Income

4 Ways to Make More Money

I've always said the best way to make more money is to work more with the clients you already have. Work with the ones who love your work, trust your judgment and have already given you their business. It's also much less work than going out there and finding new clients. Sometimes just by offering more to existing clients and not even doing full-blown sales sessions, you can make tons. It made me about $20,000 the first year I gave it a try.

Here are four ways you can make more money without spending any money at all.

■ After Sales

Just do them. No excuses. No nothing. The first year I attempted this, I did nothing more than make some price lists and email them to my clients with a little note saying, "Hey, you can add this stuff on if you want." Boom! I had an extra $20,000 in my bank account after the first year.

The best part about this, however, isn't even the money. It's the fact that I'm now providing a full photography service to my clients. Without blatantly offering things like wall art, album upgrades, parent gifts and so on, you're leaving your clients with empty spots on their walls or CVS prints as their only options. Give them the option of you providing everything they want, rather than them trying to do it all themselves.

■ Increase Your Profit Margin

One of the scariest things for business owners is raising their prices. I tell people to raise their prices consistently, and specifically every time someone books their highest package. But did you know that you can make more money without raising your prices?

This will require a little bit of math and analysis on your part. If you don't already know your cost of sales and cost of business, check out the free tutorial at bit.ly/joypricing. You'll need to know both for this quick money-making exercise.

Another good idea is to take a look at your expenses. It's incredible how much money you spend that you don't even realize you're spending. I like to keep track of my books in 17Hats and QuickBooks Online.

Once you have your data, it's actually fairly simple. Cut costs. I'm not telling you to cut quality, but find areas that you can stop hemorrhaging money for things you probably don't need. Cutting costs allows you to make more money per job without the fear of raising your prices. As long as you do it in a way that doesn't noticeably change your level of quality, it'll probably be a good move for your bottom line.

■ Exclusive Products

Business owners have to compete with the widening scope of products that are easily available to consumers these days. While you can preach until the cows come home about the difference between the canvases you give and the ones that they can snag with a Groupon, sometimes you just can't sway them.

A sure way to overcome this is by having products that clients absolutely cannot get anywhere else, such as deep matte paper, acrylic prints, metals and specialty frames that can only be found at professional printing labs like Millers. Feel free to embellish on the products as well. I like having my clients feel the deep matte paper and comment on how it feels like their pictures are printed on rose petals. It'll be hard for them to Google that one!

Make Them Fall In Love

Thankfully, if you're photographing weddings, so this is an easy one because your clients are love-minded already. Your job is simply to transfer that feeling to your products. This last tip is almost a no-brainer, but I see so many people not taking advantage of this simple idea.

Post your printed work. We get to create absolutely gorgeous displays. Canvases, albums, prints — whatever! Whenever you get a product in, photograph it and post it on your social media. Make a blog post about your products and maybe even have a gallery on your website showcasing them. It doesn't have to be crazy. To be honest, I just snap a few shots with my iPhone half the time.

Displaying the types of things that clients can do with your photos will help them start to fall in love with them long before you ever get them in front of your camera. It'll also show off your work in new ways and may even make a difference whether to book you.

Personally, I have a gallery dedicated to "Albums & Art" on www.vanessajoy.com, and I direct new leads to it when they inquire. I also mention it to my clients a few months before their wedding. By the time they come in for their album session, they're fairly well educated on what I have to offer. They usually have an item or two on their must-have list.

■ It Doesn't Stop After the Wedding

Bonus tip! Why not re-offer products to your clients for their one-year anniversary? Thanks to my 17Hats workflow, I have an automatic email sent to all of my couples on their first-year anniversary giving them a 25% off coupon to their online gallery, just in case they still have some photos they want to print. It takes me no time at all (literally zero), and it's just an offer they can take or leave, so I don't feel pushy about it. Find ways to boost sales after the event for a little extra on the bottom line.

If you're a studio that does repeat business, then use this same methodology to encourage clients to come in to update their family photos, headshot or whatever type of photography they originally came in for. Alternatively, two years after the wedding you can do what I do and casually mention that I do maternity photos as well. Whatever works for you to get them in your door again.

Following these tips are a sure way to bring up your bank account sooner rather than later and with positive long-term effects as well. Use this time to make some changes in your business and boost marketing efforts!

Easy Photo and Video for Wedding and Event Professionals

"It's so easy my iPhone can do it." But then you get a real camera.

Wedding and event professionals are more frequently using professional camera gear to capture photos and videos. Whether you're using it for marketing purposes or selling a product or service to your clients, learning photography is likely in your future. I've been a wedding business owner for the past 18 years, and I'm here to help you learn the photo/video basics.

First things first. You're likely going to be shooting in a primarily dark location. This means you'll need a little more than just a camera that shoots both photo and video. I personally recommend the Canon 6D Mark II. It's a great camera at a good price that'll give you the low light functionality you need for both photo and video.

Aside from a camera, you'll want two things: a flash and a tripod. The flash will be for shooting photos in a dark reception hall. The tripod will hold your camera still for solid video shots. For the flash, you'll want to invest in a solid one with easy auto-functionality like the new Canon 470EX-AI, which has an auto-moving head that will determine the best bounce light angle. It takes all of the guesswork out of it for you.

The tripod won't be used heavily, so something lightweight and sturdy is all you really need. Something light and collapsible like the MeFoto RoadTrip will be an easy addition to your arsenal without breaking the bank. If you want to move around the dancefloor, a small gimble like the Zhiyun Crane 2 will do the trick.

Alright, enough of the gear. Onto the process.

Let's start with photos first. Photography is a whole field in itself, but I want to make this easy for you so that you just get moving with it. The best thing to do is to utilize your camera and flash's intelligence as much as possible. Since you'll primarily be shooting in a dark environment, I recommend either setting your camera to the P mode (it'll just do everything for you) or the Tv mode. In Tv mode, set your ISO to 1600, 2000 or 3200, depending on how dark it is in the room (the darker the room, the higher the number) and your shutter speed to 125 in a darker room or 250 in a brighter room. After that, the camera will do the rest for you. For your flash, I very much recommend the Auto-Intelligent bounce flash because it will instantly give a more professional look to your images without you having to learn a thing.

For the video, your settings will be a little bit different. I don't recommend P mode because it will adjust things a bit too much on its own. You could use Tv mode and set your ISO to 1600, 2000 or 3200, depending on how dark it is in the room (again, the darker the room, the higher the number) and then set your shutter speed to 50. The best way to use video is to shoot in Manual mode. A good work-around would be to use Tv mode, look at the suggested settings and then dial them in manually. Either way, stay still on a tripod or gimble so that your video is clean and not shaky.

Doing something with the pictures afterward doesn't have to be a pain. Take the photo and video clips and then mash them together in an easy editing program like Animoto (tutorial there for you!) for a quick social media marketing piece, new content for your website, or even a gift for your client. You'll have tons of photos for social media and print marketing, plus video clips that can be used in myriad ways. Happy shooting!

How to Attract Couples During Engagement Season

For Wedding Professionals, around New Year is the most wonderful time of the year. Why? A ton of couples get engaged over the holidays, particularly on New Year Eve. Maybe it's because these proposing guys are just so inspired by the holiday spirit, or perhaps they're just trying to combine events so they can remember the dates.

Regardless of the reason, my research on Google found that almost 30% of proposals are between Thanksgiving and New Year's Day, around one million proposals in just a short amount of time.

After the initial excitement of getting engaged wears off, the wedding planning begins, and brides and grooms everywhere are looking for their wedding vendors. What can you do during this time of the year to make sure that couples searching for business owners find you in the huge sea of wedding professionals? How can you put yourself out there and be found by couples who will book your services?

You can follow four steps to make sure that you're doing your best to attract this new influx of couples.

1. Maximize your marketing efforts
2. Brush up on your SEO
3. Spend advertising dollars wisely
4. Make your website work for you

Maximize Your Marketing Efforts

Marketing is the way that you communicate your goods and services to potential customers. It's important to note that marketing does not need to be synonymous with advertising. We'll cover advertising, which generally costs more money, in another step.

Be creative with your marketing plan. Think of ways to reach your target market that will seem natural and not an obtrusive form of advertising. No one likes being sold to, but everyone likes feeling like they magically discovered your amazing work as if it were the best-kept secret since who shot Kennedy. So find ways to let them discover you.

One of my favorite ways to market to future couples is to hold a Facebook Photo Contest. By celebrating my previous year's couples by entering them in a photo contest, I let them spread the word about it to all of their friends and family while I watch the likes on my Facebook Fan Page go up dramatically.

Be sure to follow Facebook's rules on holding contests. Facebook doesn't allow their "like" button to be used as a voting or entry mechanism in any type of contest or promotion (more on that here). You need to use a third-party application to host the contest for you.

Here are some more third-party photo contest applications I found online:

- Offer Pop
- Woo Box
- North Social
- Photo Contest App

The key is letting your clients spread the word for you. Email or Facebook message your clients with a simple text to copy and paste so they can easily tweet, post and email it to friends and family. Having them do the work for you is not only easier, but it takes you out of the equation, thereby making the whole thing not look like an advertising ploy. Make sure you have intriguing prizes that will get your clients excited about it and inspire them to really want to win the contest.

Consider these fun prize ideas:

- Free Mini Photo Session
- Dinner and a Movie Date Night (www.restaurant.com and www.fandango.com gift certificates shipped with a bottle of wine)
- Complimentary Bouquet
- iPod with their wedding film installed

■ Brush up on Your SEO

Google is undoubtedly one of the best tools for finding anything in the world, and couples searching for their wedding vendors are sure to use it. Search Engine Optimization (SEO) is the key to making sure that your company shows up in her search. There are volumes of information out there on SEO and how to make it work for your business, so if you're not already making this a priority, now is definitely the time to start.

Check out these resources for learning and implementing SEO in your business:

- http://www.tofurious.com/business owners-seo/seo-for-business owners/
- http://www.business owners-seo.com/

■ Spend Advertising Dollars Wisely

Ultimately, you should also invest in advertising for your business. Most business books will tell you that you should put at least 10% of profits back into advertising. You want to make sure that these marketing dollars work for you and that you spend them in the best possible way. This requires some research for what works in your area, demographic and target market, and some straight trial and error for what works for you personally. The best way to make this efficient is to keep good track of where your leads and bookings are coming from. Using a client management system like Tave.com, PixiFi.com or ShootQ.com will make this very easy.

At the end of every year, take a look at last year's leads and bookings. What advertising methods are bringing in leads but not bookings, leads and bookings, or no leads or bookings? For your advertising dollars to be worth what you're spending, they should bring in at least a Return on Investment (ROI) of three times the invested amount. Whatever isn't doing this for you, get rid of it and try something else with those dollars.

What if you're just starting out and don't have the budget for high-priced and traditional advertising means like print ads, bridal shows, pay-to-play reception hall vendor lists, or wedding website listings (The Knot, Wedding Wire, etc.)? You're not lost! Here are some low-budget but extremely effective ways to spend advertising dollars.

▪ Vendor Brochures

As a business owner you have what every other wedding vendor wants and needs: amazing photographs of their work. Put together a small, 4x5, double-sided print press card that has a nice collage of your photos of their work, along with both of your logos and contact information. Give 25-100 of them to any wedding vendor that you want to work with more frequently and that attracts the kind of couple you're looking for. What reception hall wouldn't give out free brochures with their work on it to every prospective couple that walks in the door?

▪ Blog Advertising:

Advertising with smaller, but prominent wedding blogs, can be effective and a much less expensive option than advertising with larger wedding websites like The Knot. For some blogs, you have to be accepted before being permitted to advertise with them, like Style Me Pretty, but it's definitely worth a try. Blogs like Green Wedding Shoes, The Knotty Bride and Wedding Chicks are a great place to start.

■ Referrals

If you already have relationships with fellow business owners, hopefully you've created a nice networking circle where you each refer jobs to each other when one of you isn't available for the job. If not, consider developing those relationships or offering a business owner in your area a finder's fee if they refer a job to you and you book it. No business owner can work every wedding, and I can't imagine too many of them would mind making a few bucks off the weddings that they can't work.

■ Make your website work for you

All your marketing, SEO and advertising efforts will be useless if or when you finally get these new couples to navigate to your website, and you present them with a website that's messy, clumsy and not your best first impression.

There are a ton of different ways to attract new clients your way and I hope this has given you a few new methods to try. Varying up your marketing and trying new ideas will keep you fresh and in front of potential clients continually.

similar advice, but if you take one thing from this topic, make sure that your good relationships and good name matter a lot in this business. You don't know whether this caterer has a cousin who runs the biggest bridal magazine in your area, but you do know that you have to work with this caterer today. How you react when they ask for a few photos of the food from tonight may have an impact down the road.

You can take it a step further, though. If you know from the bridal magazines that certain vendors just always seem to have their work featured, get to know them on purpose! See how you can collaborate, maybe by doing a photoshoot for them, and talk to them about how they get their work into magazines. They may be thrilled to introduce you to someone, and your path just got a lot quicker to that publication.

Still want more tips to grow your photography business, become confident in your marketing skills, and get those first photos featured on the glossy pages of a bridal magazine? Visit www.BreatheYourPassion.com to learn more, and of course, follow me on Instagram (@VanessaJoy) to get to know my work and how you can reach your goals as a photographer!

What Makes a Luxury Brand? 5 Ways to Raise Value and Justify Charging More

When I ask business owners if they'd like to make more money and work less, I rarely get no for an answer. The response I usually get is, "Tell me how." After all, who doesn't want to create a better product for their clients and get paid more for it?

The secret behind creating a luxury, boutique-style brand isn't classified information. In fact, it's fairly obvious because most of us know what to expect when we walk into a high-end retail location. If you don't, take the time to walk into a luxury boutique clothing store or pretend you're buying a car at a Porsche dealership. You'll soon see that the methods behind a high-end approach are out there for all to see.

Before you take my word on it, I'm going to be very real with you. Last year (from when I wrote this) I photographed 20 client weddings, ranging from $6,821 to $18,482, with an average spending of $11,379.15 in an area where the average price paid for a business owner is $4,000 to $5,500. With my couples spending more than double the average wedding photography price, I know a thing or two about a luxury brand.

Show Me The Wow

Truth be told, this is where the rubber meets the road. The start-to-finish experience you give your clients either holds your brand true to its word or becomes exposed for what it is. Your brand sets the expectations for your clients, and you have to follow through with it 110%.

One way I keep up my brand image through my client experience is with client gifting. I want my clients to feel special, and I want their decision to go with me to be validated throughout our time together. Better yet, I want to give them tangible items to share on social media and to brag to their friends about, furthering establishing my brand, its recognition and reputation. I give them a "Hello" gift, a "Goodbye" gift and an "It's Almost Your Wedding Day" gift. Gifting is one of my favorite love languages, so I relish in showering my clients with surprise presents.

However, you want your clients to remember your business and how you want them to share it with friends and family is how you'll want to tailor their experience. Do you tout yourself on being an expert in your field? Then continually offer tips and tricks to your customers. Is your business about quality of life? Then look for ways to help improve your client's well-being outside of the service or product you're providing. Go above and beyond for your clients in a way that superbly represents your brand mission, and you won't go wrong.

Don't Blink

I remember when I first started charging for my work. I was 15 years old at the time, and a realtor wanted headshots. So I set up my white backdrop (I had no idea how to light it, by the way) and got my exposure on my Canon 10D. I then promised the client that we would keep taking pictures until we got one she liked and thought she could use. All for $50. I remember cringing when I told her that's what I would charge her.

Spouting off the number in your price list may not be the most natural thing in the world and that's ok. However, that doesn't excuse you from learning how to confidently give your pricing to your prospective clients. You must learn to state what you charge without hesitation. If you hesitate, so will they. But if it's easy for you to say, it'll be easier for them to pay.

Along those lines, be extremely careful about discounting. Luxury brands don't discount. Christian Louboutin shoes are almost never on sale, and even if they are, it's not the staple shoe design that everyone wants. When you walk into Gucci or Prada on 5th Ave in New York City, you're not going to find clearance racks. And if you did, shopping on them would almost be considered tacky.

If you want to throw in something additional for your clients to sweeten the deal, then offer them a "gift" rather than a discount. Gifts come from friends and family, but discounts come from used car salesmen.

■ Shopaholics Rejoice

You want your clients to value the product and service you're offering them, especially if you run a boutique business and are charging a premium for it. Part of being able to get your customers to pay your luxury price is conveying to your clients that you value what you're offering.

When you're selling high-end fashion apparel, you cannot try to sell it while wearing off-the-rack. You need to wear staple pieces from high-end brands to be convincing to your clients and to relate to them as well. Too bad clothes aren't typically a tax-deductible purchase. When you're selling your product and want your clients to pay top dollar for it, then you have to show that you treasure what they treasure. For example, I hang professional pictures of me and my family up in my studio space and talk on social media about my next planned time on the other side of the camera.

Even more specifically, the brands you buy, wear and show support for says a lot about the kind of person you are and what your business is an extension of (more on that later). Political affiliations aside (though not to belittle the effect that can have on business), the brands and type of brands you visibly support will communicate one thing or another to your audience. Make sure that it's communicating that your brand is luxury from start to finish.

Would You Smile Already?

When I do my initial consult with clients, I always tell them about my second business owners that will accompany me to a wedding. I stress to them that not only do I care about them being about to produce quality imagery, but I also look for people with similar personalities and demeanor to me as well. If I'm trying to get my clients to "pay me for who I am rather than what I do," then who I am needs to be seen in my personnel as well.

One of the biggest day-of perks my couples experience is that I am calm, collected and seemingly in control the entire time. Even when everything is going haywire, I'm still smiling just as any experienced luxury business owner should be. Being a rock for my clients is part of my brand and indicates the experience I want my clients to have, so every member of my team needs to know how to do the same.

Who Are You?

If you're a business owner, this is ultimately what a luxury boutique brand is about. You are the face of the company, and you are what makes it unique. The best part about this is that you can simply build the luxury brand around who you are. In fact, the most well-branded small businesses I've seen are ones where the owner has done exactly that. A high-end wedding planner I know, who is an Anthropoligie nut with Restoration Hardware all over her house, became wildly successful by making her business an extension of herself and her personal and home lifestyle.

It seems like a no-brainer, but it's amazing how many people I've seen attempt to create a business that's the opposite of who they are. One of two things will happen in that case. Either the business owner changes who they are to be a reflection of their business, or there's a disconnect between the owner and the brand that leaves clients subconsciously confused.

Take Steve Jobs, for example. That man looked, dressed and acted like everything we know the luxury brand Apple to be. He was simple and sleek with an intelligent sophistication about him. He practically was a black iPhone. Could you imagine if he were the opposite? If he wore Free People clothing and acted like a flower child? Or if all of a sudden he took up the hipster trend and traded his black shirts and almost wireless glasses for plaid and thick frames? He wouldn't be Apple anymore, and there would be a huge disconnect with the brand. A luxury brand doesn't have loose ends. Everything, and I mean everything, is strategically placed in a beautifully decorated and presented package.

This isn't to say that you need to script your life. In fact, it's just the opposite because when you make your business about you, all of the above will easily fall into place because it's just you being you. To quote Gary Vaynerchuk in his book Crush It, "Watch me for two seconds and you know exactly who I am and what I stand for. Authenticity is key… I'm not putting on a performance when I do the show or my blog spots—I'm just being me."

Luxury branding is a continuous task that evolves as your company grows. Currently, I'm working on creating a new brand at www.BreatheYourPassion.com, and I'm starting from the ground up. You can create or adjust your brand at any time. That's one of the best parts about owning your own business. What you do can be as small as the type of post-it notes you use or as large as the billboard space you just rented. If I were to sum it up, these three words perfectly describe the basis of luxury branding. Just be you. Start with you, end with you and be true to you everywhere in between.

Running Your Studio

Get Out There: How to Set Up Your Studio for Success When You're Not There

So you own your own business. Congratulations! Owning your own photography studio is just one of the best things out there. You get to make your own hours, be your own boss, live life the way you want. Right? Then why do so many of us have trouble leaving the studio? Why does our chest tighten up at the thought of not checking email every hour? What makes it so impossible to think of ever having a real vacation again?

Many business owners struggle to get outside the studio, whether for a vacation, staycation, or a long weekend. Heck, even to do something for work, like attend ShutterFest or photograph a destination wedding, can be a logistical nightmare.

It doesn't have to be. I recently spent six weeks in Brazil completely away from my studio, and aside from the typical readjustment back into life in the good old U.S. of A., my photography business didn't suffer. In addition to outsourcing, which I've previously discussed, here are some guidelines I used while traveling to take my first Tim Ferris style mini-retirement.

Set the Rules

Truth be told, you'll probably have to work while you're away, but you don't have to let it consume your time. Know the bare minimum that you'll need to do to avoid a massive pile awaits you at home. More importantly, know how much you'll need to do so that you can relax if you're on vacation or how much you'll need to work if you're on a work trip. When I travel to photography conferences, I know I'll have minimal time to get work done, so I just do only what is absolutely necessary in the morning and make sure I stick to that every day I'm away.

Make Yourself Mobile

If you're traveling, you might not always be able (or want) to plop down with your laptop and get to work. Know this ahead of time and prepare for it by setting your work up on your cell phone. Emails and phone calls are a no brainer, but make sure you have access to things like:

Your Calendar

I use Google Calendar for everything. I love the integration it has with my iPhone through an app called Tiny Calendar.

Your Client Management System

I currently use www.Tave.com, but I also love Sprout Studio and 17 Hats.

Your Documents

I use Google Drive to keep track of things like my ShutterMag articles, and I always have quick access to my favorite images and personal items like meal plans and tax documents.

Your Email Templates

Text Expander is a life-saver in my company. They have a mobile version that allows me to quickly respond to inquiries and send contracts while on the road.

Have Access to Home

This is a two-fold system for me. First, I use www.logmein.com to be able to quickly access my home computer and anything on it. Aside from that, I host all of my images, including backups, finished album designs and other completed graphics, on www.SmugMug.com. This allows me (or anyone else in my studio) to be able to access any images or designs I need. I can place orders for my clients from anywhere in the world. This is also particularly helpful when I have a magazine or blog editor asking me for a couple of specific pictures I've taken that year. I can easily provide them with a download link to a gallery I created for them or pull images they need and send them over.

Schedule It Like Anything Else

Isn't it amazing how easily we can schedule work appointments like shoots, consults and sales sessions, and then we wonder why we don't have time for friends and family? Time with friends and family, and especially time away from the studio, has to be scheduled like any other work appointment, or it will easily get thrown by the wayside.

I make sure I schedule time for things like the gym, church and when my parents come to visit. If you plan on being away from your studio, put it in your calendar and schedule things around it. I also don't recommend scheduling calls or Skype sessions until you've settled in wherever you'll be and know what the internet and your daily routine will be like there. The last thing you want is to be overcommitted, which will lead to you being overwhelmed and unable to relax or do your job well.

Leave The Gear

It's natural as a business owner to want to bring everything you have with you. I get it. I'm a total gear geek myself. When you're traveling, especially on a plane, you'll need to be more selective about what you bring. If I want to bring lights on the road, I thank my lucky stars for my Profoto B2s. If I have to shoot a job, I'm not going to bring every lens in my repertoire, no matter how much I want to. When I shoot destination weddings, I typically bring just my Canon 50mm 1.2, 135mm 2.0 and 24mm 1.4 to cover my bases (and maybe a macro lens). To see what gear I typically have in my bag, head to my YouTube channel for more of what gear I currently use (www.youtube.com/vanessajoy).

If you're not going to shoot a job, then it's up to you to decide what gear you're going to bring. For me, I just bring my iPhone. I know, I know, I'm a horrible hobby business owner at this point. I just can't stand carrying heavy gear with me. I don't even like carrying a purse if I can help it.

Check out the video to see how I spent six weeks in Brazil and what kind of gear I traveled with. Pre-warning, I shot this video self-style!

Moving From Weddings to After-Marriage Events

Among the list of irritating comments that I got while pregnant, one was, "Oh, you're going to start photographing babies now!" Um, no. Why? Maybe it was the hormones, but I still don't see why just because something is present in my life that I will have the immediate passion to photograph it in other people's lives. I mean, I don't photograph dogs or birthday parties, and I have plenty of those going on around me. Or, maybe it was the business owner in me trying to teach others that different genres of photography are different art forms that need additional skills and time to master. Whatever it is, I'm not photographing babies—I even have someone else photograph mine.

However, there has been a slight expansion in my business as of late, and I've grown to enjoy it. Throughout the years I have photographed a maternity session here and there when a former bride asked me, but for the most part I've referred clients who ask for portrait sessions to other business owners. It may be because I was pregnant, so now I see more of the beauty in pregnant women and understand how to photograph them better.

To be honest, I think it's more convenience, though. I found a few factors that made it easy for me to add maternity sessions to my repertoire, and it's been beneficial in more ways than one. Here's a quick how-to from my thought process and how I started getting my maternity work off the ground.

Take Baby Steps

I felt that maternity photography wasn't a far stretch from weddings because the focus of the shoot is still a woman. Truth be told, many times I could do without the groom and have a field day just photographing the bride in all her bridal beauty. Photographing women has always been something I loved. I love making women feel beautiful, and out of all women who need to feel beautiful, it's the ones who are creating another human being (but more on that later). So it wasn't a far stretch from photographing brides to photographing the next stage in their lives—having children.

Moving from weddings to maternity photography was only natural and made marketing easy because I already had the clientele. It's akin to starting a wedding photography business when all of your friends are getting married. Weddings are simply happening all around you, so word-of-mouth is easy to spark. One of the first things I did was simply send a short email to my past clients, letting them know about my new venture. That simple task alone brought in quite a few leads immediately. I booked my next gig. That strategy got me a ton of congratulations, built up my relationship with current clients and expanded my brand. All the hard work that you've done marketing your wedding business is going to pay off double if you use that same group of people to target for maternity photography.

Be Conscious of Your Lifestyle

Here's the kicker: Maternity photography can be done during the week so that I can continue to focus on weddings on the weekends, or (gasp) I may have a weekend off! Having a new baby in the house, I can't help but wonder what it will be like when she is five and six-years-old and wants me to come to her soccer games on the weekends, but I can't because I have to work. It's not that I have any plans to stop wedding photography at this point, but if I did, I'd want to know that I ready have one foot in the door. It's just smart to have an exit strategy or secondary backup plan for whatever type of work you're doing at the moment.

Price Yourself Right

Portrait pricing isn't something that I'm wildly experienced in, but since starting after sales a couple of years ago, I definitely have a better idea of where to start. I took a look at what my engagement session packages looked like (you're welcome to view them here www.vanessajoy.com/engagement-collections), and I based my portrait packages off of that. I also did my due diligence in making sure that I talked to different portrait business owners around the area to make sure that my pricing for sessions was on point as well. I didn't want to be that business owner who was undercutting the industry, and at the same time because I do have a higher-end brand and price point for the weddings I do, I needed my portrait offerings to reflect that as well.

In regard to giving out or selling the digital files, while I do give digital files in my higher packages or à la carte for my weddings, I knew that it wasn't something I wanted to do for portraits. Portraits are supposed to be hung, put in a book, or given out as gifts. I knew that if I just offered my clients digital files alone as an option they would choose that, and the photos would never see the light of day.

I will say that of all the advice that I got, I learned a lot. Just like wedding photography, it can be very hard to compare apples to apples, and it seems everyone simply does whatever suits them—which is great. However, the same concepts apply to portrait pricing as they do to any other kind of pricing. You have to figure out your cost of sales first. You must figure out how much you want to make per hour. Do the math and add it all together to figure out what you need to charge to make what you need to sustain your business and your lifestyle. If you want to learn more about that, there's a short video that explains the math behind it here: bit.ly/joypricing.

Regardless, when figuring out how to price yourself with portraits, definitely ask advice from your fellow business owners in the area. Don't be sneaky and pretend to be a client, asking for pricing through their website. There so many groups on Facebook and other amazing photography communities (like this one) where you can ask experienced portrait business owners for their advice. I recommend that you construct your packages similarly to your wedding packages. This will be an added benefit for your past clients as they will already be familiar with your package structure.

All in all, I'm excited to dive into the world of portrait photography. I know so many business owners who make a beautiful living photographing portraits and nothing else. It is indeed a lucrative way to apply your skill-set and photography in many ways, ensuring a continual flow of business. If you're already photographing weddings, then it's that much easier.

Price Yourself 4 Ways to Put a Pep in your Business Step

I was sitting at a bar with my husband last night. He's a wedding cinematographer and has been one for the past 20 years. I've been a wedding business owner for the past 18 or so, so we have similar ideas on a career in weddings and what it means to do this for a living, day in and day out.

While talking to him, it made me realize just how prevalent the burnout factor is in photography and not just in photography, but in any creative field. I feel like our world is oversaturated with creatives right now who haven't yet begun to understand the burnout factor. The start-up culture is still fresh and young and thriving, and I think soon we will see the effects of burnout.

What can you do to make sure this doesn't happen to you? First of all, you can't prevent it. It will happen to you. If you look at statistics for businesses, about 80% of them fail in the first year, and then another 80% of those that had succeeded failed within the next five years. And if you don't fail, then you'll likely hit a few snags that'll spiral you a bit downward in your creative state. I can certainly understand that, not just in terms of how hard you have to work, but because you'll be trying to find a way not to be bored of what you're doing every single day.

It's not easy to be a self-starter and conjure up a work ethic that could rival pretty much anyone's. But then, to add creativity on top of it and then to be creative on demand? It's a magic formula that very few people figure out.

I want you to be successful, not just in photography, but in life as well. Here are ways that I've discovered have helped me in photography and owning my own business.

1. Be Creative

I know that sounds silly, especially since I just finished telling you about the woes of being creative on demand, but the truth is, creativity is in our blood, and it's a strength of ours. However, that does not mean that our creative muscles can be stagnant for years without getting weak. Being creative requires work and constant flexing of our creativity. It requires exploring, experimenting, and, yes, even failing. In fact, just today I tried something new in the studio and pretty much landed flat on my face in front a client. Oh well, moving on.

The best thing I can tell you to do is look outside of your industry or your genre of photography for inspiration. If you're a portrait business owner, look at weddings. If you're a wedding business owner, look at fashion photography. If you're a children's business owner, maybe look at food photography. Whatever it is, step outside what you typically do and draw inspiration from sources you're not familiar with.

Personally, one of my goals this year is to bring a lot of portrait techniques and skills into wedding photography. Hopefully, it will be some stuff that will not only spark my creativity but give me a little bit of an edge in my portfolio by showing off things that are typically not seen in wedding photography. If you'd like a little posing inspiration, go to: bit.ly/2DMLUdm.

2. Be Lazy

Okay, I don't actually mean for you to be lazy, but I thought it was a good title because a lot of us think that taking a break means we're being lazy. If that's what you think, then you know what? Be lazy, because you need to have a break. I always look with fondness on the Jewish community for seriously taking a Sabbath day every single week. In fact, their old law says that someone who does not take a Sabbath day should be stoned to death outside the camp. Thankfully, I don't think they do that anymore, but it's certainly a strong statement for the need to rest.

It's not just about the rest. It's not about you necessarily sitting down on the couch with your feet up and a bottle of wine next to you, although that does sound great. It could mean that you're spending time with family, friends and working on relationships and things outside of work, which need just as much, if not more, attention than the things inside of work. By making sure that you take rest, you're not only strengthening your world outside of work, but you're strengthening yourself as well.

The book Getting Things Done, by David Allen, which I highly recommend you read, by the way, stresses the fact that being bored is necessary for creativity. When our mind is relaxed, that's when you can be your most creative self, and that's when you come up with a ton of ideas. This is why there's a market for pad and paper that you can write on while wet. We're forced to be relaxed in the shower, assuming you're not listening to an audiobook, as I do, and you get a lot of ideas while you're there.

3. Push Yourself

It's easy to be a business owner and find a bit of success or even make a living at it, and then quickly grow stagnant. I'm a firm believer in being content but never complacent. Complacency leads to being bored, and that boredom can lead to dissatisfaction. Therefore, I find it really helpful to have big, long-term projects or goals that you are actively working on. I'm not talking about those big, long-term goals that you just hope to happen one day. I'm talking about the ones where you sit down and make a plan in order to get there by a certain date.

In EntreLeadership, Dave Ramsey talks about goals not truly being goals unless you have an actionable plan to achieve them. If you don't have that plan, then they're just dreams. So find something that you want to be, do, or have within the next one or two years, and make a plan to reach that goal. Break down your plan by months or weeks and do things that move you closer every single time.

Sometimes it takes a thousand little steps to get to the top, or sometimes it might take just five big steps. Whatever it is, keep yourself pushing ahead and wanting more, but at the same time, always be content and grateful for what you have. Having goals and pushing yourself forward should never be the product of envy or looking around at your competition. It should be something that comes from within, something that you want for yourself and are willing to work for.

4. Call for Help

Friends, use your support system. It's amazing how perfect everyone's lives look on social media. I myself admit that I try to paint a pretty picture. Social media has us thinking that everyone else has it all together, but trust me, no one has it all together. It's always the ones that portray the most perfect life that have the messiest house on the inside. After all, we want a nice clear, great brand online that exudes professionalism and, of course, high-quality photography.

But that doesn't mean you can't admit your struggles. Yes, even on your business social media accounts. It's amazing how much true support you get when you lead an open dialogue about your struggles to those closest to you or even to those online.

I think it's wise to have close friends that you can confide in, and I, of course, have those, in addition to my husband. These people, maybe two or three of them, see the real me and every nitty-gritty thing that I go through. But that doesn't mean that you can't reach out to your acquaintances or to your audience online for some light support as well.

I don't recommend writing huge sob stories or taking advantage of this in any kind of frequent matter, but sometimes all you need are a few "Atta boys." Or a couple "Keep your head up" comments. It's all you need to push yourself through whatever burnout or struggle you're going through. Not to mention that a little honesty online will probably inspire others to do the same. And who knows? Maybe by the time our children grow up, or my children grow up, we won't have to worry too much about how detrimental social media is to society. (Hey, wishful thinking, I know.)

I hope these tips have helped you find a way to push through burnout in your photography career. Try one of them or try all of them, but just keep moving forward. I'm going to leave you with a quote that I have hanging up in my office by Martin Luther King Jr. "If you can't fly, then run. If you can't run, then walk. If you can't walk, then crawl, but whatever you do, you have to keep moving forward."

End of Wedding Season Push

If you're a seasoned wedding business owner, you already know that the last quarter of the season can get tough. Maybe you took on too many weddings this year, or maybe you feel a bit of longing as the end of the wedding season is in sight. Whatever it is, wedding professionals typically look forward to a little bit of a break come winter—unless you're in warmer climates, then you're just getting started!

In the northeast, weddings in September and October tend to be the most beautiful ones because of the pleasant temperatures and bright colors. The last thing we want to give our clients is a tired-out business owner. Here are my tips to making it through the last stretch of the wedding season.

■ Throw Out The Cookie Cutters

At this point in the season you've perfected your wedding routine. You can do your work with your eyes closed, and nothing can surprise you the day of the wedding. This is, of course, a good thing, but it can also lead to some serious boredom.

Do yourself a favor and pick up your favorite fashion magazine, or scour the internet for new ideas that you can try in your last few weddings of the year, even if it's a freebie for the client. Now is the time to throw a few curveballs into your game since you have the basics down pat and let's face it, future clients need a little inspiration to step out of the cookie cutter Pinterest style. It'll help give your work a style that doesn't look exactly like everything you've done that year, which will be great for social media as well.

As I write this, I'm getting ready to attend a two-day workshop to give myself a boost that I'm in dire need of. I can't wait to get those creative juices flowing and bring new techniques to my remaining weddings this year!

■ Avoid Burnout

Burnout happens when we've been doing something for too long or when we've been doing it without taking a break. I feel it toward the end of the season, and I know I'm not alone. If you're finding yourself getting irritated easily, or if you're tired or frustrated, you're probably getting close to burnout. Don't wait until you actually roll your eyes in front of your bride when she asks you to copy that stupid Pinterest picture. Deal with your burnout before then.

The best thing you can do, whether you're already in burnout mode or if you feel yourself inching toward it, is to take a break. Some professionals like to stay within their craft, but they do something more creative with it that's outside of paid work. Others, like me, need to put the camera away and completely detach from the wedding world. Get a massage, take a nap in a park or just spend a day binging Netflix shows and eating chocolate. Whatever gets you the recharge you need to give your couples your best work and your best you.

Here's the big key to this step: you must not feel guilty about this off time. For a long time I felt a great deal of shame when I took days off. Consequently, it made the time I took off completely useless because my body may have rested, but my mind didn't.

Human beings are not built to keep on working without a break. In fact, breaks and boredom are what give our minds the free space to be creative, come up with ideas and get inspired. Even my friend and fellow business owner, the workaholic Sal Cincotta, can attest to this because he'll admit to nightly laying his head down to rest and then when his mind and body have been given that break, that's when his best ideas start flowing. Rest! Good things will come of it.

▌ Keep it at 100%

It's very easy to start slacking off at the end of the year. Along with having a well-established shooting routine comes a little bit of laziness. Many of the wedding procedures become second nature for you, so it's tempting to be a bit lackadaisical later in the season. If you give in to that mindset, however, that's when things start slipping.

Often, I'll see this happen, not at the wedding itself, but with the workflow before and after. When things appear simple, it's easier to procrastinate rather than when there is a little bit of pressure. If you have staff, now is a good time to get them motivated as well, so they don't slack off either.

There are lots of ways to motivate yourself and your team. I'm a huge fan of giving things to look forward to, such as an end-of-year party or surprising them with little gifts here and there. It's motivating for me to give of myself or my money, and I know they love the sentiment behind anything we do. This is not to mention that the things we do together are great for team-building and studio morale.

Having staff meetings are another good way to boost efforts. Keeping your team in-the-know about how the company is doing, what goals have been reached and which goals still lie ahead are wonderful ways to keep everyone on the same page and working toward pushing the company forward together. Even if you're a team of one, sitting down and looking at the year as a whole will motivate you.

If you do have some staff, even if it's just second shooters, I highly recommend reading the book EntreLeadership by Dave Ramsey. It's chock full of amazing business advice with everything from financial advice to ethical guidelines. The sections on team building are solid, and after reading it you'll be quite anxious to start implanting the ideas in your own photography studio.

Often enough, the end-of-the-year burnout comes from taking on too much work. While having work is a blessing, it can also be a curse. One of the earliest decisions I made in my business was to make sure I wasn't overloading myself with weddings because I didn't want to have a short career. Doing too much is a quick way to find yourself wishing away photography from your life.

If you think you're overworked, you're likely being underappreciated as well—and most times you're the one undervaluing yourself. The best cure for both of these problems is to (gasp) raise your prices. You and your business owner are worth the raise, your clients are worth you not hating working their wedding, and your family and friends are worth the free time you'll be able to spend with them. Time is your most valuable, limited asset. Make sure it's going to something of value at all times.

Cultivating Your Support Network

Make Friends, Friends: The Networking Secrets of Business

It's amazing to me that the wedding and event industry continually develops and adapts. I'm so proud to be a part of such an incredible community and to have the privilege of watching it grow. In 2020, I would even say it was a privilege being a part of the event industry as it fell and suffered due to COVID-19, because so much good came from that when you look at the ways we all built each other up during such a trying time.

The secret to all business is this: It's about relationships. The good ones and, yes, even the bad ones. The bad ones drive and motivate us to do things like start a magazine. The good ones encourage and support us like friends who help us start literally from the ground up (like the hotel ballroom floor Sal and I sat on when he told me his idea and I pledged my support).

"It's not about what you know. It's about who you know." I used to say that with a twinge of bitterness in my mouth, thinking that only the well-connected would benefit. Now, a decade or so later, I realize that it isn't a snide statement. It's a wise bit of advice. The best thing you can do in business is to expand your network.

Ok, enough of the reminiscing and theoretical talk. Let's get down to it. If so much of our success sits on the shoulders of who we know, then it's our job to get out there and expand our reach. Here's how you do that.

1. Get Uncomfortable

This year I spoke at a Wedding Gown Specialist convention. Obscure, I know. But those people need social media advice too, and that's what I was there to teach.

A conference full of Wedding Gown Preservationists meant one thing to me. I knew absolutely no one. Not a single soul. Not even the person that flew me out there to speak (we had only corresponded via email).

There I was at the opening night mixer. I dressed as best I could—confident but not intimidating—and walked into the ballroom. Omgosh, where is the bar?! My heart was ready to burst out of my chest as I surveyed the room. I had no idea what on earth I was going to say to anyone, so I held my breath, walked to the nearest circle of people talking amongst themselves and said, "Hi, my name is Vanessa."

I didn't stay long talking to anyone, so it didn't get that awkward. When the convo died, I simply excused myself and found another group to do the same thing with. By the end of the night, I had met at least half of the people there. No, I didn't remember their names (I should work on that!), but the next day when I had to teach them, I knew a lot of smiling faces. By the time the next night's party came around I felt like I was out with friends.

Shy? Me too. If that story made you sweat, you are not alone. Success with new relationships doesn't come from how comfortable you are meeting new people. Success comes from you getting out there regardless of how you feel. Pivot.

2. Shut Up And Listen

The next step to building relationships is to simply to stop talking. Really. I don't care if you're meeting someone on Instagram or in person. If you want to start the relationship right, at least act like you give a damn about the other person.

It's not brain surgery. People like to talk about themselves. They like to brag and have people gush over them. So, give them the opportunity for both. Ask questions about what they do, how they started, what motivates them, and what they're most proud of in their life right now. Anything works. Well, maybe not politics—but hey, even that may work in the right scenario.

When you do talk, make sure you replace the number of times you typically use the word "I" in your dialogue with the number of times you use their name. According to Dale Carnegie's book How to Win Friends and Influence People, the sweetest sound to anyone's ear is that of their own name. Just be sure not to overdo it like this guy I went out with once did. "Vanessa, why don't you, Vanessa, tell me what Vanessa likes to do on the weekend, Vanessa." We didn't go out again.

3. Be The Next Lunchroom Cool Table

One of the first times I went to a big wedding convention I remember feeling like I was back in high school. I was never at the cool kid's table then, and I certainly am not at the cool kid's table at conventions either.

In fact, I remember once sitting in a room with a couple of speakers from the show just watching how they interacted with one another like old friends having the time of their life. I wondered, How could I get in with that group? Then it dawned on me. I couldn't. At least not to the extent that they already were friends. I didn't have the history they had together.

Instead, I realized that it was never about getting into the cool kids' club. It was about forming your own. Now, I don't look up to find friends; rather, I look across to find colleagues to form friendships with that'll last a lifetime. I make my own circle, and you can too. You can do the same thing with wedding vendors in your area, with families, with any kind of business relationship that you can imagine.

Be your own cool kid's club. Develop relationships over time that will help your business grow as you help theirs grow.

Long-Term Plans

▍ How Will You Be Better This Year?

At the end of every year we reflect on our goals for the upcoming year. We have tons of hope for the coming year and lots of forgiveness for the past year's failures. We wonder if we will really change this year. Will this year actually be the year that we see our business double? Or will this be another year where, in the end, you forgive yourself for not really crushing it the way you know you should have, but you'll promise to do better next year?

Friends (and I mean that because only friends tell each other the truth), it is very likely that you will fail miserably at all of the "goals" that you've just set for yourself. Why? Because they're not actually goals, they're dreams. And dreams are nice, but they're not actionable. Dreams are precursors to goals, and goals only happen when you have the balls to make them happen. Make no mistake, success does not fall in your lap.

Success IS NOT a result of the perfect New Year's Resolution. Success comes from hard f-ing work. It's the kind of work that throws a wrench in your personal life. The work that does not stop day in and day out. Work that causes the magical equation where one day off equals one month of making up for it. But most of all, it's the work that we don't want to do.

I know you think you're a business owner and you do work that you love and blah blah blah. But here's the truth: work that leads to success is so often work that you do not want to do. So here is a list of things that you need to do this year that 100% suck.

■ Go to The Gym

Yep — that's right. I know you thought that I would start off ripping some work-ethic stuff in your face, but nope, I didn't. Why? Because before you were a business person, before you ever dreamed of starting a wedding event business, you were a human. You are human. And humans need a few things before they can do anything else.

Your well-being matters more than anything else. If you can't get up, you can't work. If you can't feel good about yourself, you can't be creative. If you're not taking care of yourself, it's impossible to take care of your clients.

Personally, I have two favorites that fit my lifestyle. I love Beachbody (just ask ShutterMag writer Michael Corsentino about this—he got me hooked on Liift 4). I can do these exercises in my own home, in my own time. And I love yoga—www.yogaforphotographers.com, which works great for anyone in the wedding industry, is something I created. I need to maintain strength with Beachbody workouts for carrying heavy camera gear, and then I need to balance myself, not just mentally but physically, by putting my body back together through yoga.

Do whatever works for you, but do something and know that if you give your body the finger, eventually it's going to give it right back to you, and at that point you'll need something a lot lighter than a mirrorless to keep working.

Cut the Crap

Here is a list of things for you to cut out of your life faster than greased lightning.

- Friends that enable you to be lazy or stupid
- Family that doesn't support you
- Your excuses
- Your excuses that you think are reasons
- Your reasons for not pushing forward
- Time killers. I know Game of Thrones is waiting in your queue, but if you don't win your business throne during the week, then you don't get to watch GOT on the weekend.
- Social Media. Get off it unless you're working. And treat yourself to paying someone to do it for you for just one month this year.

Announce Your Goals

Nothing gets you closer to your goals than accountability. Make what you want public. Ask for what you want from the people who can give it to you. Choose someone that you have to tell about your failures.

And don't make this a publicity stunt moment. This isn't about getting anything off your chest and it's not about attracting some sympathy or support. It's about you creating a tangible goal, defining a timeline for working on it and facing the fact that if you don't meet those goals and micro goals, it's your fault and no one else's.

Get Good Things in Your Life

I told you to cut a lot out, but you'll want to replace it with good things. Here are some things to actively find this month.

- **Support**: Friends and family that support and slightly intimidate you into moving forward
- **Sleep:** Yep, sleep. I like the Calm app and Somalunex for my crazy insomnia.
- **Time Boosters**: Find ways to get more than one thing done at a time or get things done faster.
- **A Positivity List**: I am not a dream-board building, positive-vibes chanting bite of crunchy granola. However, there is so much negativity thrown our way, and we spend way more time believing it than we should. Recently, I've started taking screenshots of positive things people say to me and saving them in an album on my phone. It's a conscious choice to believe those things versus the negative things. Make that choice for yourself.

I know this is a massive list of things you do not want to do, things you never feel like doing, and things that will never inspire you to roll out of bed in the morning. But because these things are the hard things is exactly why they are the things that will make you successful. Anyone can roll over and do the easy stuff, and that's why everyone isn't going to make it the way you will if you work the hard stuff. If you don't want to look back this time next year and regretfully and shamefully "forgive yourself" for not reaching your goals, then it's time to make these changes. No excuses, friends.

End of the Year Panic

What happens when it's the end of the month or the end of the year and you're nowhere near your booking quota? Panic sets in, right?

You're not alone. You might even be wondering if this month or year will be your last in your business. Even in my busiest booking years, I had this kind of fear set in right before the new year rolled around.

You don't have to be scared. You probably need to analyze a few things. But if you've been doing what you need to do as a business owner all year, it's unlikely that you're about to meet your demise. Here are a few tips I've learned along the way.

Keep Good Records

Odds are you're right around the same number of booked weddings that you were at this time last year. We just don't remember it. Keep good records using your client management system (I use 17Hats) so that you can look back on this. I can't tell you how often my husband and I have had this discussion, where one of us is freaking out, but then we look at our numbers and realize we're right where we need to be.

What Have You Done Differently?

Have you raised your prices? Then you should know the number of jobs you can book and still make the same income.

Have you cut back on advertising, marketing or social media efforts? Hey, now you can see the effect of that route. Now it's time to dial it up a notch.

Have you lost focus on making your clients 110% happy? Treating your clients like the gold they are will always ensure they send you new business.

Know Current Booking Trends

When I first started my own business back in 2008, it was typical for a couple to book their business owner 12-18 months out. Now, for a multitude of reasons, the booking trends have shifted, and I typically book my clients 8-12 months in advance. Take that into account when you're looking at your expected bookings. And take heart, after all — engagement season is now through Valentine's Day, and a lot of people plan same-year weddings nowadays.

If you think about it, we're the lucky ones. How many other working people can see months and months ahead of time that they're going to have a change in income and still have the chance to do something about it? Around the US, two weeks is the standard pink slip notice, and you have much more warning than that if your bookings are in fact experiencing a decline.

The last thing you want to do with this information is to blame it on the industry or anything else out of your control. That won't do you or your business any good, and your mortgage company certainly won't be taking excuses for payment next year. If there are things you need to change, do it now.

Not sure where to start? Check out www.BreatheYourPassion.com for both free and paid marketing videos that are sure to help.

Will You Be an Old Fart Wedding/Event Professional?

When I was first entering the wedding industry, I was about 20 years old. I remember going to my very first photography meet-up. It was in the back room at the Peter Pank Diner, and there were about 25 men and me. The industry has certainly changed since then, but one thing I remember from the more seasoned professionals was the fear of not being able to "do weddings when I'm 60."

Hey, weddings take a toll on your body for sure, so much so that I've even made it a point to work on the longevity of my body (more on that at www.YogaforPhotographers.com). I mean, how many of us have disability insurance in place just in case we're injured and can't work for a while? I know I don't—it's crazy expensive!

I was recently ridiculed for using the term "minimum wage." The stupid Troll thought I was saying that people should be paid less than what he deemed s "living-wage." It wasn't what I was saying at all, but it did get me to start thinking a bit. How many serious, full-time professional business owners aren't paying themselves a real living wage?

In the wedding world especially, it's easy for us to think we're making a ton of money as we take in a lot of money. The problem is that we take in that money and then need to spend it elsewhere. When was the last time you took a look at your costs of sales and cost of business? How much time do you spend working? We end up making a lot less than we think we do. At times, we realize that there's no way we've set ourselves up for the future. It almost makes you wish you had that 9-to-5 and 401K!

You may run your numbers and think, "I'm doing pretty good." But now I want you to take that number of how much you make per year (after all of your expenses) and then divide it by how many hours you worked to get it. Are you making a living wage or just minimum wage?

A living wage should mean that you can save for retirement, and I believe that's where a lot of us fall short. Let's face it, the wedding industry is a tough business. It's stressful, we work long hours, we have lots of equipment expenses, and it's physically strenuous. Are you prepared to retire one day? Or are you hoping to have a second career?

Saving for retirement is no easy task. It is a task that takes a serious amount of planning and a lot of diligence over a long time. Dave Ramsey (I'm a huge fan of this financial guy) would suggest that we save 15% of our income for retirement every year. That seems like a huge number when you're currently saving 0%. But you want to know what an even bigger number is? The amount of money you need to have in your retirement fund to retire.

Chris Hogan (a colleague of Dave Ramsey's and the author of Everyday Millionaire) says that "Retirement isn't an age, it's a number." Do you want to see what your number is? Go take his Retirement IQ quiz here: https://www.chrishogan360.com/riq/. Shocked? I sure was!

Depressed? Ha! Yeah, that's normal too. I didn't want to write the article to make you all doom and gloom, but I did want to light a fire under your ass. I mean, no one talks about this! Maybe it's because we truly love what we do so much that we can't picture ever not doing it. I get that, and I'm actually with you on it. But, that doesn't mean one day you won't want to travel more, work a little less and spend most of your time with the people you love versus the people that pay you.

Guess what's the best part of all this. You have control, my friend! You own your own business, so you can immediately make adjustments to start cutting spending and increasing income so you can start down the retirement track—even if you just started in the photography business! It's never too late to start, and it's never too early either.

I've found a lot of answers to business and personal finances in two books: EntreLeadership and The Total Money Makeover, both by Dave Ramsey. I use tons of his advice in my photography business as well as in my home life. You may or may not like him, but the advice is pretty good. Another favorite is Jordan Page. She has a great YouTube channel full of advice on budgeting, getting out of debt, and why you need seven bank accounts (um…no, not for me, but she does have a point).

Believe it or not, most financial to-do's are the same in business as they are in life. I follow the Dave Ramsey principles because they work for a lot of people and for me. However, they're not for everyone, and some investors would even tell you that they're entirely backward. I know that finance has to do with math, but it has more to do with behavior than anything else. Here are the basic principles I live by in my business for everything:

1. **Know your numbers**. There's no excuse for not knowing how much money you have, will have and will have to pay out. If you don't have the means to figure it out yourself in QuickBooks or 17Hats, hire a bookkeeper in addition to your accountant (sometimes they're the same person).

2. **Never go into debt**. for anything. I've made it a habit of thinking about my purchases in terms of whole numbers. If I want to buy a lens and it's $1,000, I'd like to pay $1,000. Not $1,235 after I'm done with interest when I forget to pay it off in the six-months-same-as-cash deal. Paying more for things than necessary is a quick way to lose in your financial life. Equipment, staff, and even cars are all paid for in cash based on what I can afford to buy. If I want something bigger and better, then I wait until I've saved up the money for it.

3. Plan for the unknown. This may sound morbid, but plan for things like injury and death. I have three to six months of expenses saved up just in case of an emergency. The last thing you want to do while your boat is sinking is to pour more water into it by going into debt (I think that's a Dave Ramsey metaphor). In addition, if you have people that depend on you, get term life insurance that's 5-10x your salary. You never know, and it's better to leave a blessing behind than a burden.

If you don't feel like doing a ton of research on getting your financial house in order, no worries. Check out the video for this chapter where I outline the first steps to take to financial freedom. You'll be hitting your goals in no time and saying goodbye to financial stress and the thought of being forced to work until you die. Unless you're me and look forward to that kind of thing.

PART 2

Branding Your Business

Getting Back on Track

Everyone knows that it takes hard work to get to the top of your industry. Building a business is no joke, and the amount of work you have to do to get to your desired level of success is often overwhelming. What most people don't talk about is the fact that once you "make it," you have to work just as hard to stay where you are.

So what happens when you've realized just a little too late that you've been falling behind? Whether intentionally or not, slacking off has serious consequences. Making up for lost time can result in double the effort needed to bring things back to life. So what can you do to double-back and get things back on track?

Boost Your Social Media Efforts

Social media is a great tool, but in a way it relies on momentum, and if you've halted that for whatever reason, it takes a lot of energy to get it going again. Go back to the basics with your social media, concentrating on the platform where your audience is primarily. Do you shoot weddings? Then focus on Instagram. Are families your thing? Try being more active on Facebook. Perhaps seniors are where it's at? Then get yourself going on Snap Chat.

The last thing you want to do if you've already found yourself in a rut is to half-ass the comeback effort. So, don't just sign onto your social media network of choice and haphazardly post when or what you think you should. Do yourself a favor and reeducate yourself on the platform. Some things have likely changed. You'll also probably discover different ways to use things you've already been doing that'll be more effective for you.

Secondly, get into a habit of scheduling your posts. Personally, I'm a fan of Buffer because I like the format, and I enjoy looking back at my analytics time and time again. Other systems like Hootsuite, Meet Edger and EveryPost might be more up your alley. Whatever you do, make sure you're planning out your posts to be consistent and as highly effective as possible. You won't see the change right away, but after you build up enough momentum, you'll start making up for lost time.

Concentrate on Networking

Just like in everyday life, if you don't put effort into relationships, they tend to fall apart. The same goes for your business relationships. Odds are, if you've fallen behind, this is one of the areas that got hurt the most.

Take the time to look back at your wedding industry contacts and simply touch base with them. Send a friendly note. Maybe even one that includes a nice Starbucks coffee gift card to perk up their Monday. Do whatever it takes to reconnect and let them know you're still there.

In addition to this, one of the best things to do at any point in your business is reaching out to new people. I recently did this when I decided to develop more relationships in the higher-end New York City wedding market. I attended a networking event full of the who's-who in the wedding world, and I did my best. I actually ended up having to ditch the people I went with (just for a few moments—don't worry, I didn't bail completely) so that I would force myself to have the nerve to walk up to perfect strangers and start having a conversation.

And what do you know—it worked! I made a great connection with a prominent business owner who invited me to his Instagram pod, where I'm now connected with more amazing wedding vendors. I also was able to get a personal invitation to check out The Plaza's biggest competition near Central Park. Nothing has paid off in dollars yet, but I know it will ten-fold.

Get out of your comfort zone and boldly find a way to network with other businesses in your field. Be careful to do this tactfully. After all, no one likes a cold call or spam email sent their way. But find a way to do this right and it'll seriously boost your reputation in the business.

Experiment With New Tactics

Odds are, if you've been out of the marketing world for a little while, things have changed, as they tend to do so rapidly. You'll likely find that things that were working for you previously aren't working anymore. Welcome to the wonderful world of marketing in the twenty-first century!

Luckily, basic marketing principles stay the same because when it comes down to it, you're still dealing with people. And we're all subject to basic psychology. Marketing is really just tapping into that psychology to make what you offer align what they need. Grab yourself some marketing books and do some reading on basic marketing if you're not familiar with this concept. I have a few to recommend on www.breatheyourpassion.com.

But to learn the most up to date marketing tactics, I actually don't recommend picking up a book. By the time books are printed and distributed, half of the "new" marketing ideas are old news. Instead, search through business and marketing blogs, not even necessarily in the wedding industry world. Do a few Google searches on the social media platform you want to concentrate on. Follow social media marketing gurus like Gary Vaynerchuk.

Finally, you can't really go wrong by checking out what other people are doing successfully. I know when I want to find new marketing ideas for the wedding world, I'll look at top wedding blogs, wedding dress designer Instagram accounts and the like. It's a great form of research looking at how their audience (which is similar to mine) reacts to their newest post and marketing efforts. I'm not saying to steal anything, but find inspiration and adapt it to experiment in your own company.

If you have ever heard me speak at a conference, you likely know that my big takeaways are usually the fact that you have to work for what you earn. If you've fallen behind, then let me be the first to tell you you're going to have to work harder than most people around you to make up for it. Take my advice on getting back on track. But then, once you're where you need to be, never let yourself fall behind again. Work hard, work smart and work until you're motivated.

Social vs. Market Norms: How Treating Your Clients and Employees Defines Your Business

Gift-giving is a great opportunity for wedding and event professionals to show their appreciation and build their business. So what do you get everybody? And what does your gift say to those receiving it? Is there a difference between giving them a monetary bonus or a gift of the same value? Does either set a precedent for how you run your business?

Dan Ariely, author of Predictably Irrational, would say it does, and I agree. Think about it. We all know the Starbucks effect, right? Homey atmosphere and okay coffee make a multi-million-dollar company. What's the key there? Or better yet, why is Dunkin' Donuts, whose atmosphere feels a little like a cafeteria (and which thrives on speedy service, especially now with their drive-through), also a wildly successful coffee business?

The truth behind this is found by seeing how a business is run by social or market norms. Social norms are behaviors and practices learned and executed in social environments with friends, family and community. For example, social norm expectations occur when a friend asks you for a reasonable favor, and you, of course, oblige without expecting anything in return. In fact, you're happy to do it. It makes you feel good to help out.

Market norms are the opposite. They are behaviors and practices learned and executed in other types of relationships, such as those formed between business colleagues or during retail exchanges, etc. You pay $1.50 for a pack of M&M's, and you get that pack of M&M's. Nothing more, nothing less. There is no emotion attached to the exchange. You get what you pay for and follow the rules to an almost mathematical effect.

So what? Aren't "norms" just psychological mumbo jumbo? Well, in a way, yes, I suppose. But that mumbo jumbo done correctly has made companies like Starbucks and Dunkin Donuts so successful.

What do you expect when you go to Starbucks? How about when you go to Dunkin' Donuts? You expect two complete opposites, right? Starbucks is about the fuzzy feeling you get when you walk in and sit in a couch chair with your logo-ed paper cup in hand. Dunkin' Donuts is about fast service. Get in and get out. Both are great to you, and when given that kind of service in each respective location, you're happy because that's what you expect.

But what happens if Starbucks replaced their warm fuzzy feeling with the fast, get-in-get-out-type of service one day? Or Dunkin' Donuts made you wait ten minutes in the drive-through but delivered your coffee with a hearty smile? Neither situation would sit okay with you. Why? Because these companies have the norms of their business firmly set. Starbucks is primarily based on social norms, while Dunkin' Donuts is primarily based on market norms.

The $15 Lesson

How does that transfer over to your business? Why does it matter at all, and why can't we have a little bit of both in our business? I'll tell you a little story about how market and social norms came crashing together in my own experience.

I was about one year into my business. I tried following all of the examples of the business owners that I admired, and I built my business mostly with the social norm perspective (though I didn't know it at the time). I was friendly, took on a limited number of weddings at a higher price and aimed to under-promise and over-deliver to all of my clients, thereby surpassing their expectations.

Around Christmas time that year, a client of mine wanted to use a photo for her Christmas card and asked me for the digital file. To answer her, I pointed her to her online gallery where she can purchase a $15 med-resolution file of the image that would work just fine. She was pissed. And it was over fifteen dollars.

After many emails back and forth, some very heated, with me explaining these were my "policies," and the price was a lot less than she'd pay most business owners who would insist she order the Christmas cards through them, we finally just came to a stalemate. To tell you the truth, I don't even remember how the issue was resolved, but what I do remember is being completely baffled as to why $15 was such an issue. $15! That's like, ten packs of gum. Come on!

Why was $15 such an issue? Because sticking to my "policies" over such a small amount of money made me look like the Gestapo and the exact opposite of what I had presented myself as up until that point. It was the complete opposite of what I had told this bride to expect from me (through my previous actions). I was building my business on social norms, and then threw my market norms in her face when it suited me best. As Dan Ariely said in his book, Predictably Irrational, "My advice is to remember that you can't have it both ways. You can't treat your customers like family one moment and then treat them impersonally—or even worse, as a nuisance…—a moment later when this becomes more convenient or profitable."

What I did ultimately, after venting my problem on an online forum and getting no good answers, was simply to raise my prices by $100 (the average sale I got from online downloads/prints per job at the time) and to vow next time just to give my client the silly file. Win-win. I make the same amount of money (or more really, since most clients don't ask me for photos like that and just buy them in their online gallery). And I keep my client happy and stick to the social norms that I built my business on. This also explains why, in most cases, social norm businesses (or "boutique-style" as it's popularly called right now) are priced higher than a market-norm business. We all have to ultimately put the same food on our tables at the end of the day; it's just how you go about building your business that makes the difference.

You can now see how setting social or market norms can greatly affect the atmosphere of your business, as well as help you manage, meet and even exceed client expectations. These norms will determine how your business will run.

Setting The Tone For Your Staff

However, this mumbo jumbo isn't just for your clients. It's for your staff as well.

Why are companies like Google breaking all sorts of records for business and development? Do they pay their employees overtime and make them all work 80 hours a week? Are they threatening their employees with quick deadlines and the thought of losing their jobs? Not quite.

In most jobs, especially 40 or 50 years ago, market-norm exchanges governed them. Think of a factory setting. At the 5 o'clock whistle, everyone drops what they're doing and leaves. You worked 40 hours, so you got paid for 40 hours. Market norms.

You can probably imagine that Google does not run on market norms. They're the leading company of social norms. They're re-writing the book on it. Just click here to check out what the "Googleplex" has to offer all of Google's employees, for free: http://computer.howstuffworks.com/googleplex1.htm. Free gourmet food, free haircuts, places to work out, play video games, you name it. Who wouldn't want to work there? And who wouldn't mind spending more than their required 40 hours a week there or thinking about work when they're not there.

By using social norms with their staff to blur the line between work and pleasure, Google has created an amazing and wildly successful company. Ariely noticed, "It's remarkable how much work companies can get out of people when social norms (such as the excitement of building something together) are stronger than market norms (such as salaries stepping up with each promotion)." Social norms create motivation and loyalty in staff.

As you were reading through this chapter, I hope you've started analyzing your business and its relations with clients and staff. In what ways do you follow social norms? In what ways do you follow market norms? How can you use these norms to create the type of business atmosphere and work environment you want? Or if you're already mostly rooted in one of the two but want to change, how can you change the business you have from a social- to market-norms business or vice-versa?

My advice would be to start with that gift, especially during the holidays. What better time to turn things around than the holidays and the start of the New Year? With your staff, say you want to spend $25 on each of them. If you want to have a market norm workplace, then consider getting them a gift card for $25 or throwing them a bonus in their paycheck that week. They will definitely be grateful for it.

If you want to follow social norms, get them a gift worth $25. Though it has the same monetary value, and truth be told the staff member may not even like the gift really, the gift will boost your social relationship with your staff and provide the motivation and loyalty benefits that we talked about earlier. Ariely explains it best when he says, "While gifts are financially inefficient, they are an important social lubricant. Sometimes, it turns out, a waste of money can be worth a lot." You can use the same type of thinking when determining your client gifts.

There's nothing wrong with either type of business structure. Both methods can be successful when properly executed. The only real danger is mixing these norms within your business, as you saw with my complete and utter failure at it. If you're not sure which way your business is currently running, watch this video and take the short quiz to find out. You can either keep or change your business norms from there.

Business Norms Quiz

1. What do you normally call your staff?

    a. Team members

    b. Employees

2. How much info about the company goals, successes and failures do you give your staff?

    a. Need to know basis.

    b. They know what applies to them so they can get their job done.

3. Do they know the business's successes and failures?

    a. Yes

    b. No

4. What do holiday parties look like?

3 Must-have Social Media Tips

One of my favorite quotes comes from Gary Vaynerchuk's book Jab, Jab, Jab Right Hook. It is nestled in the first part of the addendum to the book at the end. The addendum is there because after he finished writing an entire book on social media and how to use it wisely, Instagram released video-posting capabilities. This release pretty much made his book instantly obsolete before it was even published.

Now, he could have complained about it. He may have even thrown his newly finished manuscript on the floor. But what he ultimately decided to do about it is write the addendum, giving more advice and tips on Instagram's video function. He started it with this attitude:

> I have bad news: Marketing is hard, and it keeps getting harder. But there's no time to mourn the past or to feel sorry for ourselves, and there's no point in self-pity anyway. It is our job as modern-day storytellers to adjust to the realities of the marketplace, because it sure as hell isn't going to slow down for us.

Even one of the great social media experts of our time gets slapped in the face by a social media change. But it is up to us to decide to get up and work through it anyway. Here's how you can do it.

Understand the Company

Anytime a social media platform changes something, I remember that the platform is really just a company. By changing their algorithms, they are actually doing their job by adapting their product to the changes of the marketplace. After all, what is their goal? The main goal of any social platform is to get users onto their platform, repeatedly and for longer periods of time.

Realizing the root of social media outlets will help you navigate their changes like a pro. If they change something that was once working, it is probably because their users have become desensitized to it or even irritated by it. Accept that the rest of the world discovered that little social media secret to the point of beating it to death, and move on.

Check out this quick video for some myths about social media: https://youtu.be/130-F3yehsE

Understand the Culture

I have only been around about three or four generations, but it is easy to notice the pattern of older generations being annoyed by the younger ones and the younger generations being misunderstood by the older ones. Older generations may complain about Millennials, but the truth is that Millennials are just a generation that has grown up seeing and hearing things that have shaped them into who they are today. Their self-absorbed social feeds are frowned upon by the generation before them in the same way that generation was frowned upon for guys having long hair and girls wearing pants.

HINT:

Millennials like videos! Click here to see how I use videos for marketing and client communication.

Ultimately, the acceptance of selfies, long hair, or girl pants is irrelevant to us as business owners. What actually matters is understanding the target culture that we are trying to reach and engaging them in a way that they not only understand but also that makes them feel understood.

Understand the Cost

I didn't mean to make this article about The Three C's to Social Media, but hey, sometimes I just get lucky!

In the fast-paced world we live in, I know I am guilty of expecting everything right now, or at least today via Amazon Prime's same-day shipping. I don't mind paying money to get what I want when I want it. But the cost I am talking about isn't money. It is time.

Sure, you will have to spend time learning about social media tactics, like the time you are spending reading this book. That is the easy part. The harder part, and the higher cost, is the amount of time you will need to spend implementing those strategies and analyzing the results. If you are trying something new online, one post isn't enough to see if it is working for you. It can take 10 or 20 posts to start to see the social snowball grow. It will take even more effort if you don't see any growth and have to go back to the drawing board.

Be okay with the time you need to play around with social media. Marketing and advertising have always been very much about trial and error. Facebook and Instagram are no exception. Test out some tips you have learned lately and see if they work. If they do, replicate it. If they don't, try and try again, my friend.

I know this chapter had a lot of overall insight instead of actionable steps to better your social media presence. Don't worry, I have more for you right here. Click on this link for a free online lesson on how to use social media properly. You can watch it now and apply it today.

Happy Learning!

4 Steps to Updating Your Social Media Strategy

"This is SO exciting!!!!"

That's what I thought when I first heard about Instagram's release of Instagram TV, or IGTV. But then I thought of what this really meant. More work. More algorithm changes. More hours of me trying to figure out what the heck I should be doing on Social Media now.

As a wedding professional, social media is one of the strongest marketing and branding tools we have at our disposal. It's also the most time-consuming task that takes us away from our true passion of running our own creative business. Right now, Instagram is the top priority for wedding businesses in the social media world because that's where most engaged couples are hanging out digitally these days. So how can you make sure that you're doing it right when everything keeps changing?

1. Never stop learning

At some point or another, I've felt the desire to give up. Not on weddings altogether, but on little pieces here and there. It's tempting to feel that way about social media and want to kiss it goodbye because you just don't want to learn something new that came along. Fight that urge, my friends. I'm not saying you have to be a master at social media, but you need to continue educating yourself and staying relevant.

2. Don't believe the Lies

It's tempting to try and find shortcuts when social media gets overwhelming. Believe me when I tell you, that won't end well. From buying followers, likes and other things you've heard that "work," how can you discern truth?

Take a look at this video for social media marketing inspiration: https://youtu.be/peH6le3oEsY

3. Understand the Truth

When it comes to social media, the heart of the matter is obvious: it's social connection. Every time you see a change come along, just remember that each of these platforms is just a corporation trying to make money by engaging users on their platform. If you remember that concept, then you can weather any change by coming back to it. Before you post, simply ask yourself, "Will my audience engage with this?" It doesn't matter how they engage with it (like, comment, watch, click, etc.), just that they do.

4. Get Help

You likely didn't enter the wonderful world of weddings because you wanted to be glued to social media all day, every day. So, streamline the process with a social media scheduling service like Planoly, Buffer, Later, Hootsuite or Meet Edgar (and I'm sure there are many others). If you can, don't feel ashamed to hire personnel to handle posting or interacting with others. Virtual Assistants and office assistants can be great for this. They will take a lot of the weight off of your shoulders so you can focus more on your clients and what you do best.

Secret Methods to Brand Your Business

This is it. This is where you have to sit down and decide who you are and who you want to be. No pressure.

Here's the thing. A lot of business owners spend a great deal of time hemming and hawing over their brand. Let me be the first to tell you, this is useless. Why? Because brands change. Your brand will evolve as you evolve as a person, as your business grows and as times change. You can create or adjust your brand at any time. That's one of the best parts about owning your own business. Now, I'm not recommending that you change your brand frequently. That would actually defeat one of the main purposes of branding (brand recognition—more on that later). A wedding industry friend of mine once told me, "Perfection is the stagnation of progress." Over-obsessing about your brand, or anything in your business, is the same thing.

Now that we have that out of the way, where do you start? I suggest starting with some inspiration. Go on Pinterest and collect ideas of things you like. Go to your favorite clothing stores or boutique shops (even the ones you can't afford but still like) and see if you notice similar colors, textures or patterns. Ideally, you'll first build your brand to resemble what you like to see, even if your work product doesn't quite match yet. Don't worry. As long as you work hard at improving your craft, you'll be able to eventually find this harmony between your photographic brand and your storefront brand.

If you're still lost, let's just start with what your website should look like. After all, your website is like your storefront, and you want to put your best face forward there. Then develop everything else to match. Take this quiz to start figuring out what you like and don't like when it comes to your brand.

1. Black background, white background or color background?
2. Circle all that apply: Classic, clean, vintage, rustic, chic, elegant, luxurious, or fancy
3. Square or Round?
4. Write four of your favorite colors here:
5. How would you describe your dream home?
6. What are some things about you that make you unique?
7. How would your friends and family describe you?
8. Pick three words to describe your style.
9. Pick three words to describe what you're going for in your business brand.

Hopefully, looking at your answers as a whole will reveal some similarities and patterns that you can use to jumpstart your brand. Take them with a grain of salt. Nothing is written in stone. It will be useful to redo this quiz once a year so you can see if there are any shifts in what you're envisioning for your company.

Building a Brand

With the way our culture is, with social media and beautiful imagery constantly being in front of our prospective clients, we can't just fake it till we make it when it comes to branding. Consumers know what a good, solid brand looks like. When a potential client looks at a wedding event company (or any company), and it isn't up to par, then the client may feel wary of the company. Even if only subconsciously. Moreover, if a company can't fulfill the entire high-end experience, there's an entire network of sites and social media that will help that client rant about that company until no one wants to work with them anymore.

Creating a boutique luxury brand doesn't start and stop at your storefront. You can do things right now to take steps toward building a boutique brand that pulls together the entire experience from the moment your clients discover you to their final farewell.

The secret behind creating a luxury boutique-style brand isn't classified information. In fact, it's fairly obvious because most of us know what to expect when we walk into a high-end retail location. If you don't, take the time to walk into a luxury boutique clothing store or pretend you're buying a car at a Porsche dealership. You'll soon see that the methods behind a high-end are out there for all to see.

Before I make you take my word on it, or on anything I say for that matter, I'm going to be very real with you. I very much believe that there is an abundance of information out there, but most of it is real dogshit. Excuse my French, but it really gets to me when I see people giving their incredible opinions on things they know very little or nothing about. Worse, it kills me to watch young aspiring business owners eat up the bad information like it's gold.

When I first started my photography business, I didn't begin by charging $10,000 and then instantly attract upscale clients and have a company that would support them. I had to work hard over eight years (and counting) and take intentional steps toward building my business, which is now averaging $10,000+ per wedding. And let me just add that in addition to the work that it took to get here, it actually almost takes more work to stay here. You will never get to the point in your business where you're waking up, rolling over and jumping into your money pile like Disney's Scrooge McDuck. Not without working hard every single day. If you do, you can write the next book, and I'll happily read it.

Wherever you are in building your business, I hope you take the time to put the legwork behind it and create a business, product, and client experience that will attract the clients you want to work with and that you'll make them happy. After all, who doesn't want to create a better product for their clients and get paid more for it?

Analyze Your Client Experience

Whether you're just starting out in business or you've been doing this for years, you need to take a second and walk through the lifecycle of your clients. Do this frequently throughout your company's life. Start with when they first contact you, when they meet with you and when they book with you. Then take a look at the engagement session and wedding, and then consider how the pictures and products are delivered from there. How often do you communicate with them, and what does that communication look like? Are you giving them high-quality everything? Do you answer their questions before they ask them? Are you surprising them or finding ways to exceed all their expectations?

Here's the thing. Your clients expect to get what you've taught them to expect. Your delivery of a good product is nothing to write home about. It's only when you find ways to exceed those expectations and give them something wow-worthy that they feel like they're getting more than their money's worth. That kind of expectation-exceeding service is also the reason they'll talk about you with their friends and family in person and, hopefully, on social media, as well.

One of the things I'm always looking to improve in my business is how I communicate with my clients. Recently, I added a new point of contact with my clients where the day before the wedding, my couples get an email that says I'm looking forward to seeing them the next day. I'll ask if they need a Starbucks run, and if so, just to let me know what they'd like and I'd pick it up for them. I've never had anyone take me up on that, but the truth is, most couples the day (and night) before their wedding are worrying about the wedding. For me to be able to jump in there and give them a little bit of reassurance—"Hey, at least the business owner's definitely showing up. She just emailed me"—that is something that I'm really happy to do. At some point, I'll probably add a little link to a blog post that

I plan on writing that talks about three ways to fall asleep when you can't sleep the night before your wedding. But that's in the future. Always innovating...

By the way, these emails are not sent manually. They are an automated email functionality of pretty much all client management systems. It's literally no sweat off your back to send them. I send emails multiple times throughout my relationship with my clients, and they are all automated through my client management system 17Hats (which you can get for free, or you can use the code "vanessajoy" to get discounted paid services). I would never recommend attempting to remember to email your couples manually the night before their wedding. That would not be very efficient.

Analyzing your client experience is a sure-fire way to make sure that you're giving your clients the high-end experience for the type of clients you want to eventually attract. Yes, of course, a lot in your business is about the product basics, but as a whole it's about so much more than that. The client experience is a mark of a luxury brand.

It's Not All Logos and Packaging

I remember one of my first introductions to branding. I was sitting in a workshop and the Nike logo popped up on the screen, and then Mercedes popped up, and then Coca-Cola. It's the most common way to explain branding. Branding is showing popular logos and letting the audience realize they have a connection to that logo, good or bad—they have a connection to that company and their product. But that's not all that branding is.

People's lives are becoming more open, and consumers are more educated on what a solid business brand should look like. Consumers are starting to have a more critical eye, and they expect a higher level of experience when spending their money. Starbucks will always redo a bad drink. Victoria's Secret will wrap your purchases like a birthday gift. Apple will forever be dedicated to a sleek and sophisticated electronic style. You need to find ways to communicate your brand to the world as these companies do.

The first thing that comes to most people's minds when they think of branding is, "What else can I put my logo on"? or "Does my website look consistent and flow nicely and with my logo?" Yes, all of that matters, but it's so much more than that. Branding is about the overall customer experience, which has so many in's and out's, places to excel and places to improve. To effectively convey your brand message to your clients, you need to look at the overall picture of what you're communicating to your audience. Walk yourself through the client process and see how they see you.

Hello Socialite

Gary Vaynerchuk writes in this book The Thank You Economy that individuals need to work on their own personal brand. He wrote this book some years ago and foreshadowed how powerful social media would become. He described how it would require that everyone create a brand for themselves. Think about how true that is today. If you find a new business or even a person that you're looking to evaluate for one reason or another, what do you do? You check out their social media, and in just a few clicks and scrolls you think you know them and what they're about.

Your customers are not the exception to this emerging social norm. When they first look at your website and want to know more about you, they'll click on your Facebook and see how many likes you have. They'll pop onto your Instagram feed and see if it looks artsy and unique but still professional. Your social media is 100% a platform for telling the world who you are, and it's one of the first ways you can convey your brand.

If you're looking to improve your social media brand presence, consider the following tips:

- Decide what you'll post about your personal life. Whatever you decide is fine, but do it intentionally one way or the other and be prepared to be judged based on it, for better or for worse.
- Clean things up. Feel free to go back in your feed and delete posts that

- aren't conducive to how you'd like to convey your brand.
- Be everywhere. Social media helps boost SEO.

How Does It Feel?

Ever experience buyer's remorse due to a product just not being all it was cracked up to be? Or, have you ever left a store with a bad taste in your mouth because of how they handled a concern or complaint? How you make your clients feel throughout their relationship with you plays a huge part in your brand and also how your customers will talk about you.

It starts with setting expectations and delivering on your promises. Don't bother promising your potential clients a great client experience if all you do for them is your job. That's not an experience—that's what they paid for. The difference between buying clothes at Target and buying clothes at Bloomingdale's is night and day because one offers an experience and one-on-one customer service while the other simply offers you clothes.

Part of your brand (and your entire business) is the experience and attention you give your clients. This doesn't just mean the formulated task list you have for everyone that walks in the door; this also includes how you handle problems as they arise, and they will arise. One of the best ways you will demonstrate what your company is about is not by how you make your clients feel while everything is hunky-dory. It's how you make them feel when everything isn't quite so peachy keen.

Things will go wrong, but you don't have to let mishaps turn into disasters. Find ways to turn your unhappy clients into your biggest advocates by addressing issues with sympathy, understanding and compensation. The experience given through the good and the bad is what your clients will tell others about and how your brand's reputation will build.

Tomato, Tomato; Potato, Potato

Communication is paramount. Don't worry. I'm not going to pick on your grammar here—although proper grammar and e-mail etiquette should be a no-brainer. However, how you speak and the words you chose to use say a lot about your brand.

For example, if you saw a website that was bright and airy and whimsically romantic and then you chatted with that company, you'd expect the same cheery personality coming through the other side of the phone, or a smiley face or two in an email. If, on the other hand, you went to a website that was more moody and dark, you'd expect to correspond with someone a bit more serious in tone.

How you speak and how you portray your personality profoundly impacts your brand because you are your brand. This isn't to say that you need to go change your personality to match your brand. It's simply to state that who you are, especially if you're running a boutique-style business and are playing an active role in front of customers, is more so what your clients are buying than the product itself. As the saying goes, "People don't pay you for how good you are at what you do. They pay you for how good you are at who you are."

Want To Come Up?

Where you meet with your clients speaks volumes about your brand and your business. Meeting at a local Starbucks or Panera? It's still imparting a brand image to your clients and you absolutely can twist it to be a positive one. If you're fortunate enough to have studio or office space, or a retail location, then you have much more control over the environment you're bringing your audience into.

Do yourself a favor and stroll in your nearest Toyota dealership. Then head down the road immediately after and waltz into a Porsche dealership. Just after taking one step in each door, you'll be met with a completely different atmosphere. Potentially, without even taking a look at the actual cars in the showroom, you'll know which car is better, or at least that's what Porsche wants you to "know." You want your clients to know, without even seeing your products, that you've got the best there is. Eventually, the reverse ends up being true, and they'll see your photos or name and correlate it to the atmospheric experience they had and draw conclusions about you and your brand from it (hopefully good ones!).

To maximize your environment, just think of the five senses and walk yourself through your space. What do you see? Messy areas or neat color-coordinated spaces? What do you hear and smell? Noisy neighbors and dinner cooking or a crackling fireplace and lit candles? Encourage taste and touch by offering them food and drinks, and invite them to hold your most luxurious products as well. Anything you can think of to positively engage the senses will create a lasting impression about your business and product.

Would You Smile Already?

As a wedding business owner, I always tell my clients about my second business owners that will accompany me on a wedding. I stress to them that not only do I care about them being about to produce quality imagery, but I also look for people with similar personalities and demeanor to me as well. If I'm trying to get my clients to "pay me for who I am rather than what I do," as I said before, then who I am needs to be seen in my personnel as well.

I often tell the story about an amazing business owner that I chose not to hire. Typically, before I hire a business owner, they come along on a test wedding, not only so I can see the work that they produce under the same circumstances that I'm shooting in, but so I can see how they work as well. Once I had a business owner join me for this on-the-job interview and, wow, did I love the images that came back.

What I didn't love was that throughout the whole day the business owner looked angry. When I addressed this, he said he was so focused on creating great imagery that he was in "the zone" and didn't realize he was coming off negatively. Ok, fine. I could accept that, so I gave him another shot. The second time around, it was unfortunately, still the same. His images were fantastic, but his ability to smile through stress was not. One of the biggest day-of perks my couples experience is that I am calm, collected and seemingly in control the entire time. Even when everything is going haywire, I'm still smiling just as any experienced luxury business owner should be. Being able to be a rock for my clients is part of my brand and something they end up raving about later. It's indicative of the experience I want my clients to have. Every member of my team needs to know how to do the same.

Let's Play Dress-Up

This may sound silly, but I have a proven track record on this one. One of the first clients I ever booked for my wedding photography business was a beautiful blond girl with an impeccable fashion sense. I met with her in person for a consultation in dress pants and a nice blouse, and it went okay. I was within her budget, and soon after she asked to meet me again with her Maid of Honor. Having already met her and knowing the fashionista she was, I chose to wear a fun fashion-forward dress and heels this time. She commented on it, more than once, saying how much she liked it when we met, and she booked with me later on that week.

What you wear and how you present yourself says a lot about your brand. You don't have to wear designer clothes necessarily, but I have found that I will relate better with my high-end clients if I am wearing high-end clothes. They'll recognize the designer brand, and I reap the benefits of that luxury brand and all it represents. The client may connect that luxury brand and what it represents with my business.

The second part of self-presentation has to do with style. Since I am my brand, I want to dress the part. Rarely will I let my clients see me in dark colors because my brand is light and airy with pastel logo colors. It may sound silly, but I've had comments on my looking like my brand, and it is not an accident that I wear a lot of light pink and turquoise colors. I wear a lot of clothes from Free People in front of my www.vanessajoy.com clients. It's all part of my Vanessa Joy brand and how I want my clients and potential clients to perceive me. This is why clothing companies will so often make their employees wear their brand. That and for the next tip below.

Chapter Checklist

- ☑ Determine your ideal brand image.
- ☑ Walk through your business and design the experience you want your clients to have.
- ☑ Apply these secrets of branding to your business.
- ☑ Just be you.

Branding for High-End Weddings

3 Things You Can Do Right Now

One of the biggest questions business owners have is, "How do you find high-end clients?" I think people expect me to have some sort of pat answer that I can give them that will tell them how to start charging $10,000 per wedding or get that couple every once in a while that spends $18,000 or $19,000 on their wedding.

The truth is, there aren't any magical steps to reaching that kind of clientele. I can't give you a sure-fire method that will guarantee you will end up having that kind of income in one year. The truth is that a lot of it has to do with finding who you are rather than finding where they are. But there are things that you can do right now to take steps toward building a high-end brand.

■ Do Marketing Research

As small business owners, we can't spend $100,000 on marketing research, but we can certainly spend a few minutes on Instagram or Pinterest. Think of the types of high-end companies that you want your company to be like, such as Free People or Anthropologie, Louis Vuitton or Gucci. These companies have $100,000+ to spend on marketing research. If you just spend a few minutes of your time looking at what they're doing on social media, hopefully you can reverse engineer a little bit of it and find some things that could work for you and your business.

In addition, you'll probably end up finding some things that will be share-worthy on your social media. After all, when you're posting on social media, you don't want to post only about yourself and your pictures. You want to post some popular content that you know your audience is going to like. Go on sites like Buzzsumo or other high-end sites you know your typical clients like, and share some of the content you think will appeal to them. It will be a great a way to reach those clients and appear more relatable to them as well.

■ Network Up

Notice that my suggestion for how to get upscale clients comes in last. That's intentional. Before you start taking on luxury weddings, you need to have the company, the product and the experience to support them. There is absolutely no point in attracting clients that you won't be able to satisfy.

When I first started my photography business, I wasn't attracting high-end clients right away. My brand at the time didn't scream luxury to the people that were there. However, my clients had friends who got engaged and were in the marketing I was trying to reach. Because I knew that, I developed this whole same-day edit process where I gave them a few pictures, even printed them, the night of the wedding. I made sure I got in front of all the guests at the wedding who were potentially getting married or who had kids who were potentially getting married sometime soon. At the same time, I worked on my brand image and raised my prices to slowly start attracting higher-end clientele.

Simultaneously, I worked like crazy to develop relationships with wedding planners, go to industry events, get published in magazines and make friends with other wedding vendors. I tried to find unique ways to stand out. For example, after a wedding, I would contact the florist and say, "Hey, would you like copies of the pictures of your floral arrangements? You can use them for your website or social media (just tag me please). And on top of it, I'd love to make you a brochure with your floral arrangements and your logo on one side." So, I'd have more pictures of their floral work, but with my logo and website on them. It was a perfect way to network, serve them and ensure they were referring me to their couples as well.

When you're trying to reach high-end clientele, there are not as many of them as there are in the average range of what people spend on weddings. To reach the fewer luxury wedding clients, you have to cast a wide net and network as much as you possibly can with unique ideas.

Wherever you are in building your business, I hope that you take the time to put the legwork behind it and create a business, product, and client experience that will attract the clients you want to work with. For more on ways to create a high-end brand, check out this video to see how pricing matches up with a high-end experience.

The Evolution of a Brand

When I first started photography, I had no idea there were different styles. I thought this picture was pretty and that picture wasn't. In a way, that's how consumers view photography. They don't know the difference between good and great photography. They usually just know the difference between good and bad, and what they like and what they don't.

There's one more aspect to wedding industry that has come into play in the recent years, and it is much more prevalent among business owners than it used to be. In fact, it's now a crucial element for all businesses, big and small. It's the brand.

For example, while most consumers don't know the difference between good and great photography when looking at a single image, they now instinctively know it when looking at a collection of images. Thanks to social media outlets like Instagram and Pinterest, most consumers have been passively trained to appreciate a good, consistent brand image. As well as to recognize a bad one.

What does that mean for business owners? It means we need to step it up a notch. I could talk to you about how to create consistent work across the board. But branding goes much deeper than that. While the surface does relate to how the product itself is presented, there are three facets not commonly discussed that you could work on.

Avoiding Brand Confusion

Ten Years ago business owners didn't have to worry about brand confusion like we do today. Consumers are better trained to see brands. Our brands are available at all times with a few clicks of a mouse or a couple taps on a phone. Most consumers subliminally recognize brand confusion, and it is something we want to avoid as business owners.

Brand confusion occurs when an out-of-norm product, post or experience happens. For example, if you're a "light and airy" business owner and you post a heavily shadowed image on your Instagram, that goes against your brand norm. Or it's when you redesign your logo or website every six months. All of these things can cause brand confusion and ultimately lead to a lack of trust in your brand from your prospective clients.

To avoid brand confusion, try these three steps:

1. Make any public changes to your business slowly, rather than abruptly.
2. Keep your brand an extension of who you are, so that consistency comes naturally.

Creating an Attractive Personality

I was recently ridiculed on a ShutterMag video by someone who claimed that pretty people with good personalities get further in life because it's easier for them. While the pretty part made me want to smack him in the face with my pretty little hand on his pretty little face, the second part of his statement is actually quite true.

The truth is, if you're a business owner, you likely deal with people. People hire you and give you money. Having a personality that makes all of those things easier for your clients is absolutely a plus, and it should be part of your brand.

Think about it. If you met a bubbly business owner, who dressed in light colors and smiled a lot, what would you guess that their imagery looked like? Dark and moody? Probably not.

Think of Steve Jobs when he was alive. He lived and breathed the Apple brand. Apple, a sleek and chic company that embraced black, white and silver as its main colors, was so greatly complemented by Jobs, who wore black every single day. On the other hand, Google is a company that loves colors and changes its logo daily, and it's a company known for an innovative, creative work environment that can be a bit off-the-wall at times. Hey, I'm all for nap spaces at work!

The term Attractive Personality comes from a book called DotCom Secrets by Russell Brunson. He talks about identifying your personality strengths so that you can use them in business. The book has little to do with the wedding industry, but it's worth the read just to hear how he talks about finding and creating your personality. Your brand has every bit to do with your personality, and it's part of what makes you relatable to your clients. And here's the best part: you can learn to have a personality.

That guy's YouTube comment irked me so much because he was picking on me for something that he thought I was just born with. The truth is I was homeschooled for nine years (9!), didn't learn social norms until way later in life, and to this day I'm not a natural social butterfly at all. I'd rather watch Netflix and chill any night of the week rather than go out and have forced conversations. Having a personality isn't something most people are born with, but it is something that most people can develop.

I knew that I had to come out of my shell to be more successful in life, so I did just that. I don't have it mastered yet, but I've learned to be more outgoing. Check out this video to see how I practice this skill in one of the weirdest places.

How to Clean Up Your Brand in 4 Easy Steps

Branding sucks. No, really, I'm just going to go ahead and say it. Branding is annoying. Branding, ironically, segregates us into a pigeonhole (where did that saying come from anyway?). And thanks to today's culture, if we don't have a distinct brand, we may as well have started photographing yesterday. Or, more annoyingly, business owners that just started photographing yesterday have better branding/presence/awareness than you, and you've been at this like a million years already.

I just finished building a Speed Posing Course for wedding photographers (www.SpeedPosing.com). I'm sitting there building the sales page and course page and blah blah blah, and do you know what really bugged me? The fact that I needed to spend more time on branding it than actually creating it.

Can I Get an Amen?

Don't worry. My rant wasn't without purpose. I want you to understand, above all, that while I'm going to teach you some branding tricks and cram all the knowledge I have down your throat, that, my friends, I'm right here with you. I feel you. I get that it's frustrating and that all you want to do is your specialty, but you wind up doing everything but that.

Now let's move on and do some work.

1. Delete, Delete, Delete

One of my favorite quotes is from Stephen King. When referring to the editing process, he recommended that one should, "Kill your darlings, kill your darlings, even when it breaks your egocentric little scribbler's heart, kill your darlings."

If you want to make yourself look amazing, take out all of the less-than-amazing. Go through your Instagram and archive photos that don't match your feed. Peruse your website and kick out a ton of images that aren't making you look amazing. When you post a blog, don't post 156 pictures of the day. Aim for 30.

Showing less means being more. It gives a more refined look to your overall brand and gives more wow to what you are showing. Just think of Will Smith in the original Men in Black—you only want the "best of the best of the best, sir!"

2. Check Yourself

For a really long time I thought that in order to be successful I needed to be a carbon copy of my successful predecessors. Wrong. So wrong. In fact, that's the quickest way to be totally boring and quickly irrelevant.

You can actually see the crazy change in my AdoramaTV series Breathe Your Passion. Look at the older episodes and then watch the latest 12 or so. You'll notice the real Vanessa Joy finally come out to say hi.

Take a look at the things you're writing on social media, the way you've written the "About me" page on your website, and the mannerisms you have when you're in front of clients. Are they wildly different from what you're really like? If so, then it's time for a change.

Now, I'm not saying that you shouldn't be more polite on jobs than you are any given morning scuttling about your kitchen, pre-coffee. Of course, you should be. I'm simply saying that if you're finding it difficult and exhausting to keep up a persona, then drop that persona. You'll have much more fun and end up with clients that are fun to be around.

3. Hire You

Ha! Wouldn't that be our dream come true? To clone ourselves and let them scurry around while we sip martinis, and roll out of bed signing autographs and taking pictures. Sign me up!

What I'm really getting at is that your brand isn't just about you. Whenever you hire another person, they represent your brand. Sure, it may only be that second business owner or assistant you hire occasionally, but your clients are watching them and judging you based on what they see.

Take it to an extreme level and note the pictures in this article. I didn't take all of them. I happened to give birth just before this wedding (yes, I did tell my clients that it was a possibility), and I was only able to come for the first look/photo session. My clients 110% fine with the possibility that I couldn't be there for their whole wedding. And can you tell which pictures I took and what pictures Jaye Kogut (my life-manager / second shooter) took? No. Not a chance. That is killer brand consistency.

4. Don't Freak Out

I know you'll likely head over to your social media accounts right now and have a mini-meltdown. Don't do that. I know we just finished complaining about other people that just seem to brand themselves perfectly the minute they open their doors, but really, that's not the norm.

Branding yourself, especially as a business owner, does not happen overnight. In fact, it takes years, and then once you've got it nailed down pat, you'll likely change because you've advanced your skills and your work shows it.

Don't freak out.

If being a business owner was all about "making it," then you'd see a lot more of us retire. The truth is that we should love the climb more than we love the idea of success. Success is like the carrot in front of the horse. I don't care who you ask. Everyone, no matter how successful they are, is always reaching for just a little bit more. Embrace that and keep climbing.

PART 3

Marketing Your Business

Compounding Your Efforts for Success, Part 1

As I write this, I'm sitting outside on my patio, enjoying the sunshine, the cool breeze and the comfort of working at home. Most people would look at my life and think, "She's lucky," but I would look at my life and think, "Damn, did I work hard to get here." It can be argued that the truth is a little bit of both, but no one can argue it happened overnight.

Whether you're starting a business, or trying to improve your life, it's always the little steps that you take that add up to major accomplishments. Gary Vaynerchuk once said that "Crushing it" does not involve a magic formula that equates to less work." Hard work will always pay off in the same way that the early bird gets the worm.

I've been reading a book called The Compound Effect by Darren Hardy, and he embraces the concept of hard work and diligence winning over talent and luck any day of the week. He refers to himself as the tortoise in the Tortoise and the Hare race. While the Hare is naturally inclined to winning races, the slow and steady Tortoise will beat him every time.

So what does this have to do with the wedding industry? Everything. It has to do with everything from your skill as a business owner, to how you find clients, to how you manage your life and how you put yourself in the position to enjoy it.

In this two-part chapter, we'll address how you can utilize the slow and steady method to win the race, as well as how to apply it to your life until you're sitting on your patio, working from home. You can do what you love with enough spare time to enjoy your life too.

Marketing the Compound Effect

I remember when I received my very first wedding inquiry from a bride who had seen my work posted on Instagram. High fives all around, right? While I was pretty proud of the inquiry itself, what I was particularly beaming over was finally seeing the results of my long-term, diligent efforts in posting and hashtagging correctly on Instagram. If you look WAY back at my Instagram feed (www.instagram.com/VanessaJoy), you'll find that the first wedding-related picture post I put up there was of a bridal bouquet from February 28, 2012. Twenty-eight months and 100's of photos later (and learning about hashtags and what to post along the way), I received my first inquiry. That, my friends, is the compound effect in action—little baby steps that amount to something big.

So how can you start creating little steps in your business that'll amount to more over time? Here are key areas of the wedding event business in which you can start taking your baby steps.

Marketing

If there's any area in the wedding event business that needs constant attention, it's marketing. Our culture changes so quickly with the advancement of social media, and consumers are getting wiser to our advertising efforts. Thankfully, making a few small improvements to your marketing strategy doesn't have to be that difficult. This year, I decided to take my social media to the next level by using an app called Later (www.later.com), which allows me to schedule posts on Google+, Facebook, Pinterest, Twitter, LinkedIn and Tumblr all at the same time without having to log onto each site. Thank you, sweet baby Jesus!

So what can you do to give your marketing a boost? How about taking five minutes a week to personally e-mail or call a vendor from the wedding you just shot and offer to give them some pictures of their venue or work? Maybe you could make an effort to post just one helpful hint a week to your brides/moms/clients via social media. Why not try utilizing a social media network that you haven't put much effort into yet and just scheduling one post a week. You could easily schedule a whole six months of posts in about twenty minutes. This way you'll get your compound effect well on its way.

Workflow

I believe workflow is another area that business owners can always find a way to improve upon. At this point, I've done so many little baby steps in my workflow that after I shoot a wedding, the rest pretty much runs itself without my direct involvement in every little thing. This reduces the stress in my life and gives me more time to shoot more, live more or love more. And it improves my overall client experience at the same time.

Think of one thing in your workflow that you hate doing. Now, find a way to make it go away.

How I truly recommend improving your workflow, however, is by finding little things to delegate to someone else (intern, office manager, or hey, maybe even your kids). Things like mailing products, shipping client gifts, and not having your bills on auto-pay add up to a sad waste of your time and talents. Find little things, one thing at a time, that won't take more than a few minutes to teach someone else and let it go.

Client Products

I would like to say that I've been giving my clients the high-quality albums, canvases and framed artwork that I'm giving to them now, but that's just not the case. When you're first starting out in the wedding industry, you simply can't afford the better stuff, so you have to settle a little. But you don't have to stay there.

Switching to a higher-end product is a bigger step. If you're not ready to do that, think about the other things that your clients receive that you can bump up a notch without breaking the bank. I give my clients complimentary thank-you cards for their wedding (complete with my logo, of course—it's almost free advertising, as your clients pay for the stamp). In the beginning the cards were smaller, less pretty 4 x 5.5 cards. Now, they're pearl-coated 5 x 5 cards with custom designs. They wow my clients and their family and friends much more. What did that change cost me? Maybe $50 per wedding, and I just raised my prices by $50 per wedding package. It's simple stuff.

Find something in your client product or experience that you can improve upon slightly and raise your prices by that slight amount. Maybe raise your prices by $25 more than what would cover your new product so that you're doubling the compound effect by bettering your client experience and making a few bucks more yourself.

We want to apply the compound effect to other areas of your life as well. After all, what's work if you can't enjoy the fruits of your labor? We want to live balanced lives because, as Darren Hardy says, we should absolutely, "Be wary of the high price of putting too much focus on any single aspect of your life, to the exclusion of everything else" (The Compound Effect).

Check out this video where I explain how I used the Compound Effect concept (before I even knew about it!) to raise my prices from charging $2,000 for my first full wedding to the upwards of $10,000 that I consistently get now.

Compounding Your Efforts for Success, Part 2

In the previous chapter I presented four ways to take baby steps to improve your business that'll lead to bigger results and positive changes in your career. In this chapter I want to take the same principles of The Compound Effect, as described by Darren Hardy in his book The Compound Effect, and show you how you can apply them to your life as well (you know, that time you have where you're not working).

Putting too much focus on our businesses is something we're all guilty of at one point or another. After all, it's easy to do. We love what we do, and we want to succeed. For that to happen, it takes a great deal of time and effort. But what good is work when you can't take a night off to enjoy a date with your spouse? Or what good is it if you're never satisfied with a day's work because you're so stressed, even to the point of having stress dreams every time you sleep?

What I didn't tell you about the Compound Effect before is that it also can work against you. Think about it. One cookie isn't so bad. One cookie every day will add up to those love handles everyone loves so much. Or consider every time you decide to ignore family for work. It may be a small decision that might impact only 15 minutes in the moment, but if you add those up over time, then the minutes stack up. You realize you've created a bad habit that'll leave your family lonely and rejected.

You can take two steps that'll help you make sure the little steps and decisions you make in your life and business are working to improve your quality of life. Pick any area in your life that you're not happy with and simply: 1. Kill the Bad and 2. Replace It with Good. Here are four main areas of life in which you can implement those two steps.

1. Family

I think family tends to be the easiest part of our lives to push to the side quietly. It's easy because these are the people closest to us that we can easily take for granted, not giving them the care they need.

One bad habit that I'd like to kill is cell phones during dinner. Think you're not guilty of it? Next time you go out with your family or sit down at home, count how many times you think of your phone or pick it up to look at it. Having a distraction like that at our fingertips causes us to fail to be present in the moment. While we're physically spending time with our family, we're mentally on an adventure somewhere else.

If this is a habit you're guilty of, then that's the Compound Effect working against you. Now, replace it with something good. Maybe leave your cell phone in the car or in another room, so there's no point in even thinking about picking it up. If you still think about it, then every time you do, let it be a reminder to you to compliment a family member who is sitting in front of you instead. Then you can watch those compliments add up to create an encouraging family environment.

2. Finances

That's right, we're going to talk about money (don't worry, no politics or religion, though!). Finances are an easily traceable way to see the Compound Effect working for or against us in our business and personal lives. This is a good thing because we can easily take a look at what we're spending money on and see in black and white how our habits are either hurting or helping us.

Go ahead; take a look at the categorical breakdown of last month's credit card statement. Not sure how you spent $584 on restaurants? I am. A little bit at a time. Think of your trips to Starbucks (don't get me wrong, I love Starbucks!). Three times a week at $4 each trip, is $12 per week, $48 per month, and $576 per year. The same compound math applies to your cable bill (which has other negative effects we won't get into), subscriptions you don't use, and office supplies you don't need.

Find areas that you can easily get rid of or cut down on, and turn it around. Make compound math work for you instead. Put that money you're saving into an IRA or other interest-bearing account, and have peace knowing after this gig is over you'll be able to retire happily. That sounds like it's worth the price of a cappuccino.

3. Friends

Remember those? You know, the friends you have that are not business owners (though don't we love a good tax-deductible networking night out?)? If it's been months since the last time you hung out with the old crew, it might be time for some friend TLC.

Making a positive change through little steps with your friends is easy. I like to schedule time with my friends just like I schedule appointments with my clients. It's the easiest way for me to commit to spending time with them and to make sure that it works in my schedule. Even if it's just once a month, take the time to schedule some time with friends. Make it a priority.

If you think you don't have the time, remember step one – Kill the Bad. Take a look at a negative, time-sucking habit you may have, such as watching TV for two hours a night (ok, I got into it) or scheduling sessions and appointments every single day of the week. Replace these habits by taking short coffee date with a friend once a month or once a week. You and your friends will be happy you did!

4. Free Time

You might be thinking, Hey, we just talked about time with family and friends. But I'm talking about free you time. The absolute easiest person to neglect is yourself. The problem is that this is where the bad compound effect can really take a toll. Eat poorly and don't take time to exercise? Enjoy that heart attack by age 45. Don't take time to decompress or take vacations (not work-cations)? Have fun getting burned out on life sooner rather than later.

This is another area of my life that I like to actually schedule. I look at the gym class schedule at the beginning of the week and put in my calendar the classes and times I want to take that week. Even if they're just 30-minute classes, 30 minutes three times a week is going to compound effect into me being much healthier than if I didn't go at all. Making time in your schedule to read or even take a nap will compound effect into me being well-rested and happier. Finding the time to relax will exponentially expand my character as well. After all, Charlie Tremendous Jones said, "You will be the same person in five years as you are today except for the people you meet and the books you read."

Taking notice at how the Compound Effect is playing either negatively or positively in your business and life can have a profound effect on the direction your life takes. It may seem like the little things you're doing aren't producing results, but I assure you they most certainly are. You have the ability to take full control over them.

Take a look at this video to hear the bad habits I've developed that have negatively affected my life and how I plan on changing them.

Instagram Growth: 5 Tips on Getting Your Engagement and Numbers Up

It's no secret that Instagram is the next (current?) biggest social media platform out there. If you're not convinced, just remember the fact that Facebook, the leading social media network, bought Instagram. Hey, if you can't beat them, buy them, right?

Depending on your type of business and your preferred style, you may not feel that your audience is on Instagram, and that's ok. However, regardless of where your audience currently is, know that eventually they'll migrate to Instagram, if for no other reason than the age demographic that it currently attracts is aging just like everyone else. More importantly, regardless of whether your target market is wildly active on the platform, a large number of consumers today judge your credibility and ability as a business based on your social media following. In other words, people are deciding whether or not to use your photographic services based on what you're doing on social media. Do I have statistics to confirm that? Not exactly. It's just my observance of the incredibly coincidental match between failing businesses and their subpar social media presence. Look for yourself if you'd like.

To prove my credibility on Instagram, feel free to check out my Instagram profile at www.instagram.com/vanessajoy. 60k followers isn't bad, and I have an average engagement rate for that number. According to one of Gary Vaynerchuk's VaynerMedia employees, I'm doing quite well and am above average. So let me let you in on some of my secrets.

Tags

The number one thing you want to do is increase visibility on your posts. One of the easiest ways to do this is to tag other accounts in the photo you post. It's best to tag people who actually have something to do with the picture. For me, if I post a wedding photo I'll tag wedding vendors as well as big brand name clothing and shoe lines that are featured. Most people appreciate the tag on the photo and mention in the description because it's a cross-promotion for them as well.

Another plus to this is that very often bigger brands and blogs will see your photo because you tagged them, and they will choose to feature you on their account because of it. Even better, I've started to see quite a few accounts actually request to be tagged in order for your work to be considered for reposting or publication (with credit, of course). Anytime you can get your work featured on another account, in front of someone else's hard-earned audience, it's a win.

Hashtags

This is an oldie but a goodie. Hashtags are still relevant today and should be used on every post. You're allowed up to 30 hashtags per image, and you need to use them wisely. While it may seem like a great idea to tag #fashionphotography in your image, you and 10 million other people had the same idea. No bueno.

For hashtags to be constructive, you need them to be noticed. I know it seems like when you use a crazy popular hashtag like #wedding you're getting your picture there in front of a billion people. But in reality, you're just throwing away your image in a garbage can full of a billion other images. Use hashtags that give your picture a longer shelf-life than 1/250th of a second. Best practices now say that 5-7 hashtags should be used.

Description Tags

Not to be confused with photo tags, these are the @ tags you write in the description or comments of a photo. In a way this is just notifying an account that you've mentioned them in a post. This is a great way to credit other people in the photo, but it's also a way of asking for interaction.

Sometimes when I use @ tags in my description, I'm tagging people I think will find the photo interesting in hopes that they engage with it by liking or commenting on the photo. Any engagement is good because it boosts the algorithm on your post to your audience. But engagement is also public, and other people can see that your post is being engaged with through Top Posts on hashtags, the Discover tab and also the Following tab. Again, be choosey with this. Trying to get @JimmyChoo's attention might not work out when there are a million other people doing the same thing.

Interaction

As with all social media, it can't always be about you. It has to be social, which means it needs to be about other people too. Everyone wants their ego stroked, and no one wants to feel like they're just being spammed for their engagement. You need to interact with other people. Be social!

Interact with people in a genuine way. Don't copy and paste comments, especially emojis, onto as many possible pictures as you can. For one, Instagram will catch onto this and block you from using the feature, or worse, disable your account. Secondly, people smell fishy a smile away. Be fresh in your comments and make sure they actually have something to do with the picture you're commenting on.

Keep in mind your target audience here as well. If you're a newborn business owner, there really isn't a point in interacting with a mom who has teenagers. Find new moms (hashtags!) and interact with them. A good way to make sure the account holder notices your interactions is to like five photos, follow them and comment on one photo, all within a minute or so. This way you'll pop up on their feed noticeably, so they'll hopefully check out your profile as well. Be careful not to do too much more than this or you'll just look like an Insta-stalker.

Cheating

There are plenty of ways to "cheat" Instagram growth. Some are completely unethical, others are borderline and some are legit. As social media continues to become more prevalent for businesses, there will be services like Social Growth Factory and Social Envy popping up everywhere, giving you an option to outsource your social media presence.

I'm a firm believer in outsourcing, but with social media, it needs to be done correctly, or the only genuineness you'll claim is looking like a genuine idiot. Buying followers, for one, is a no-no. Not only will you end up with a ton of followers that aren't your target marketing (aka marketing dollars gone down the drain), but your engagement won't match up with your follower numbers. Whenever I see someone with 20k+ followers on their account but only around 40 likes per post, I know they've paid for followers. Not cool and just plain dumb. The same concept goes for buying likes. It just won't bring more business through the door.

One way to ethically "cheat" the algorithm is to do anything new that any social platform comes out with. Naturally they want to see their new features going well, so they tend to push them in the algorithm. Instagram's Reels was a great example of this. Eventually, the algorithm does level out a bit, so be sure to jump on new features ASAP.

There is so much more that I could go into with social media and understanding it wholly. It has many facets to it, and to top it off, it's always changing. The best advice I can give you is to try and understand the root of social media companies, as I explain in it this webinar: http://bit.ly/joysocialclass.

Instagram growth takes time and effort, so don't be discouraged if you don't get the interaction you want right away. Lay the foundation by posting and interacting consistently. Keep up with it, and over time you will see a difference in your numbers.

Marketing to Millennials

The word "Millennial" just might sounds like the bad "M" word to you, but nowadays this generation comprises a huge part of the market. If you're a wedding business owner, it's your primary market. So how do you speak the Millennial language?

Being a NJ wedding business owner since about 2002, I've watched marketing methods change over the years, and I've gone through countless trial-and-error campaigns to find the success that I have now. I'm going to spare you all of the fluff in this article and get right down to what works.

Videos on social media work. Why? Millennials are on social media and most social platforms prefer video content because it keeps users on their platforms longer. And even once that algorithm trick doesn't work anymore, the psychology does. People pause for video longer than they will for photos. So here is your five-step method on how to boost your business with video.

Match Your Brand

Branding is one of the most important aspects of your business. In fact, many clients will decide not to work with you based on your brand alone. If you want a few branding secrets, download my free eBook 9 Secret Ways to Brand Your Business at bit.ly/joybrand. Consistency is key in any brand.

Make a Video

I know, I know. It seems like I just skipped 17 steps here. Trust me, I didn't. Making videos today is seriously easy. After you've taken a bunch of photo and video clips, you just need to put them together. There are a lot of programs out there to do this, and I have tried them all. Personally, I use Animoto because it's fast, easy and reliable. You can literally upload your photos and videos, click here and there, and have a finished marketing video done in 20 minutes or less.

Don't believe me? I've made you a tutorial on how to do it that you can watch for free right here. You'll watch how I make a video in less than 10 minutes and be ready to do it for yourself right afterward. Plus, I've given you a few examples of the types of marketing videos you can make on that page as well.

HINT:

You can communicate better with your existing clients via video!

Make It Compelling

Now that our world has an attention span that parallels a goldfish, it's not enough to unintentionally slap together photos and videos. You have to make it interesting enough to keep the attention of the viewer as well. There are a few tricks to doing this that'll come in handy when you're putting your film together.

First, keep it short. Keep everything short. Photos should only be on the screen for 1-3 seconds. You should have five or fewer video clips (unless something really, really interesting is happening), and the entire video should be under a minute. Under one minute ensures you can post the video on Instagram, though Facebook suggests videos be closer to 15 seconds for the best possibility of being watched all the way through.

Second, use text. 80% of people are watching your videos without their sound turned on. You need to be able to communicate your video's purpose without audio. Of course, make sure you have audio on the video (Animoto has free music included for you), but don't rely on it to convey your message.

Third, bounce the eyes. This is a great technique primarily used in cinema and TV shows that subliminally causes the viewer to be more interested (or less bored) in your video. To do this, arrange your photos, video clips and text in a way that moves around the screen. Don't position the subject of every clip in the center. Have it go from left, to bottom, to top right, to the middle, to top left and so on. Moving the viewer's eyes around the screen will keep them engaged in your video just a few seconds longer.

Post It Everywhere

Once you've created your masterpiece, it's time to share it with the world! Download the video and upload it to your social platforms directly, rather than via the share button on Animoto. This process will slightly help to boost the chance of your video being seen by more people.

At a minimum, I recommend you having a social presence on Facebook and Instagram, so post your videos there with the proper tags and hashtags. If you need some help with tricks to posting on social media, I've got just what you need right here in a FREE replay webinar chock full of social media tips.

I hope you've highlighted this chapter to death. I gave you a ton of information and a ton of homework. Truthfully, the tips and tricks I gave you here are massively responsible for the success of my business. I've booked gigs that found me on Instagram, called me and booked a $10,000 package because of methods like these. There is no end to the power of social media and using video to speak to your potential and existing clients. I've given you the tools and even more resources online. Go get 'em!

5 Social Media Marketing Myths

Social Media Marketing is one of the major ways that business owners help customers find and book their services, and many other kinds of businesses are also realizing that social media moves mountains when it comes to gaining recognition. At this point, most of us know that it's necessary, but it isn't easy, and it certainly can't be done haphazardly if you truly want to be effective. You need the creativity to create a persona and brand that people will connect to. You need to create content that people actually find relatable, unique, and worth their time.

If this seems daunting, that's okay. Because I'm here to share the things you need to know to take away your fears about social media marketing. Well, some of them. In other spots, I'm going to remind you that this, like all the other stuff, is part of the work.

MYTH - 01   YOU DON'T NEED SOCIAL MEDIA MARKETING

These days, especially in the wedding event business, you are leaving money on the table if you don't utilize social media marketing to market your business. Potential clients who are looking for wedding event professionals are often looking on their phones, using optimized-for-mobile apps like Instagram rather than surfing your website on a laptop or desktop computer. Which social media site are they on? Check the current demographics for users of social media outlets like Facebook and Instagram, Tik Tok and Snapchat to find where your target market is hanging out (and where you should be too).

No marketer ever said, "Stay with what you know and wait for the customers to come to you." Instead, you go to the customers! Create amazing Instagram, Tik Tok, or Facebook accounts that are as stellar as any website gallery. Your customers only have to "like" you or "follow" you to start considering contracting with you. I had a recent client find me on Instagram, message me on Instagram, receive my price sheet on her phone, and book her wedding with me—all without visiting my website! Make your information, resources, and evidence of your skills so mobile-friendly that you can make them shine on any social media platform.

Small side note: Just because you definitely need social media marketing doesn't mean you need every new social media site. Judge whether a site is a right match for your social media marketing strategy by whether the people you can get into your audience are actually in the market for the services you offer. This brings me to the next myth, which relates to the kinds of followers you get.

MYTH - 02   BUT I CAN JUST BUY FOLLOWERS AND LIKES

The path between no followers and 10,000 followers is an uphill climb, I'll tell you. You have to offer great content and be responsive and interactive, and it takes tons of time. So many people claim they can get all the credibility without any of the work by buying Instagram followers or likes, or using similar methods on other social media sites.

Do you want the truth? Everyone can tell if you are buying followers and likes online. They are the wrong type of followers, and they don't "like" in realistic ratios. Your followers should be somewhat interested in your style and approach if they are following you. An unintelligible username with no actual Instagram posts or profile picture probably isn't contracting with you, ever.

A good sign is that your likes-to-followers ratio is about 1-10%, meaning a reasonable number of people saw your post and thought it looked great. Not every single one of my posts is a winner with the fans, but my overall ratio proves that all 33.5k of those followers chose to like my page without being paid. This ratio gives me actual credibility. That many bots or fake accounts won't have nearly that level of engagement.

Engagement with real people who want your kind of services is what matters. Lower numbers are better than higher numbers of people who have nothing to do with your business. Wherever your numbers are, both in likes and followers, start doing your homework. Which kinds of posts get 1, 2, or 30 more likes than the others? Learn from that and grow your following.

MYTH - 03   I DON'T HAVE TO POST ALL THE TIME

You absolutely have to post regularly. This is essential so that people feel that you are a working professional with a real business that they can trust enough to sign a contract with you. Your regular posts demonstrate that this is indeed a business you take seriously. It's easy to be dubious of online businesses, so give them every reason to trust you and see you as a rock-solid investment.

As mentioned before, your social media is basically a portfolio that you have the chance to curate and add to constantly. If you are getting better as a business owner all the time (you should be!), you want to have a steady stream of new posts that showcase your skills and remind people who follow you that you are here. Post regularly and stay top-of-mind with your clients.

MYTH - 04: I HAVE TO POST ALL OF MY OWN STUFF ON MY BUSINESS SOCIAL MEDIA

Nope! Your social media posts should be relevant to your business and its potential and current clients. If something interesting to a typical wedding business owner's client, such as a popular post about three sisters having their weddings together on the same day, is going viral, then why not share it and take advantage of its innate clickiness and fun? Even though it's not your content, it's generating activity on your page, which is great for your reach.

My reach is pretty good on my own posts, but I use popular content when it makes sense. I ask readers a question, something like, "Would you want to get married on the same day with someone else?" People can weigh in when they reach the comments. Engagement breeds connection, and that keeps people visiting your page, considering your photos, and deepening their knowledge of your brand. Popular content does all that for you, as long as you have plenty of your original content in there too.

MYTH - 05: IF I DON'T DO IT MYSELF, MY SOCIAL MEDIA WILL LACK MY VOICE

Not true. You can have someone else do your social media! Pay a virtual assistant, a friend or anyone who has run a social media page before. These days, even our thirteen-year-old neighbors, kids, and grandkids are ultra-savvy when it comes to social media posts. Yes, you should get involved at the beginning to make sure the direction someone else takes your social media is a good and helpful one that maintains your voice. Once they "get it," you don't have to always be working on it yourself; you can just monitor it from there on out and make adjustments as need be. Outsource this task away from your to-do list once you see that they are posting consistently and in your style.

P.S. One more freebie when it comes to social media. Always tag other vendors. The images in anything I do collectively will be tagged to death when I post them online so I can thank everyone involved and network with them. Be sure to tag them in the photos and the description so people can find them and see the extra effort you're going through to give them proper credit for their work. Who knows, it could lead to more booking through a great vendor relationship!

Want more help with this beast that is Social Media Marketing? Check out this class, Social Media Demystified: http://bit.ly/joysocialclass. Also, follow me on Instagram @VanessaJoy to see how I use social media for my business and practice what I preach about these myths. Feel free to snag any ideas you see me experimenting with and try them out on your account. Happy Posting!

Shake It Up – How to Keep from Marketing Stagnation

It's always helpful to look back on the year to see what marketing efforts worked and then decide what to utilize again to bring in business. It's a good practice to implement. Of course, the beginning of the year is always a good time to evaluate your marketing efforts and figure out what's working and what you're wasting your time and money on. However, what can happen is that we continually do the same things repeatedly and, especially as creatives, we simply get bored with what we're doing—even if it's working fine.

There's a fine line in marketing that tells us we need to stick with what works but at the same time keep things new, fresh and interesting. As business owners, we see that two-fold with our marketing efforts as well as in our approach to product. We need to maintain consistency to keep our brand recognizable, but we need to shake things up a little to stay on top of the game and make sure that our work and business aren't getting stale. Having your marketing go stale is death to a business owner.

Here are five ways that you can liven up your marketing efforts and keep your business from becoming redundant, all while making sure that you're still leaving room to stick to the current marketing strategies that are already working for you.

1. Freshen Up Your Imagery

Marketing guru Gary Vaynerchuck tells business owners that we need to think of ourselves as media companies when it comes to our marketing efforts. This is a no-brainer for business owners because we're constantly making new media that we can use for marketing. The downside to this is that we can easily get in a rut creating the same imagery with different clients.

One way to change things up is to give yourself an imagery goal or two this year. What new setups can you learn? How can you change your typical composition for your product? Find ways to incorporate fresh elements into your imagery without changing your overall brand.

Then, use updated photos on your online portfolios on your website, wedding networks and Facebook page. Incorporate them into your daily marketing postings on places like Pinterest, Facebook and Instagram. Don't forget to use appropriate hashtags and keywords when posting.

2. Try New Paid Advertising Outlets

If you've found paid advertising sources that work for you and bring at least a three-times ROI (Return on Investment), then great! However, that doesn't mean you should stop there. You may find that other outlets can bring you just as much or more of a return. Continually experimenting with paid advertising will not only reassure you that you're getting the most bang for your buck, but it'll undoubtedly get you in front of a new audience.

Here's a quick list of different paid advertising channels that you can experiment with.

Blogs:

- Style Me Pretty
- 100 Layer Cake
- Green Wedding Shoes
- Rock n Roll Bride
- Junebug Weddings

Local And National Magazines (Consider Their Online Listings As Well As Print Advertising):

- New Jersey Bride
- Sophisticated Weddings
- Grace Ormond
- Martha Stewart
- Destination I Do

Online Advertising:

- Google AdWords
- Facebook/Instagram Ads
- Paid SEO Services
- YouTube Pre-roll Ads

Wedding Networks:

- The Knot
- Wedding Wire
- Local Bridal Show Listings

3. Make new friends

Hopefully, you work consistently on establishing relationships with similar vendors in your area. For wedding business owners, this may be local florists, event planners and reception venues. For family business owners, this could be doctor's offices, boutique clothing and toy stores and mom groups. But just because you already have great relationships with vendors doesn't mean that you should stay in your little clique exclusively.

Find ways to meet new colleagues and form new relationships. This might mean that you help a local newbie business owner in the area (that'll usually come back to you ten-fold at some point), ask a vendor whose work you admire out to coffee or establish a new connection with a unique vendor of some kind. As long as you don't have an exclusive relationship with any current vendors, there's no reason why you can't make more friends and collaborate with them on cross-promotional marketing ventures. It may even benefit you to introduce two florists that you work with to each other so they can develop a relationship and refer business, too.

4. Find New Products

When trade show season hits you have a fantastic opportunity to get out there and interact with vendors to see what's new and exciting. Updating your product line will not only give you plenty of marketing juice when you introduce them to your audience, but it'll potentially help you bring in more income when you sell these products to your clients.

Find products that you've never offered before, or improve upon the products that you currently give your clients by upgrading the quality of what you offer to them, even if it's just an extra option or perk. It'll make you look better to your clients, give them a better product and get you excited about your final delivery.

Want to take it a step further? Create a magazine featuring your newest products, offerings, even if just digitally. Here's a link to take a look at the magazine I created to show off to new leads via digital download, and print to network with other wedding vendors: bit.ly/joymagazine.

5. Beef Up Your Branding

This is a fun one! Marketing often comes in the form of how your clients perceive you and their experience throughout your time with them. By giving your branding efforts a facelift, you can wow your clients by providing them with a higher scale feeling, which will give them validation in using your services and give them a reason to chat about you.

One of my favorite ways to get my branding out in front of clients and their friends is to give client. I give them a gift when they book my services, another one shortly before their wedding, and a final gift on their one-year anniversary). Not only do I get to market my business this way, but I'm creating a better client experience, happier customers and boosting my brand in their eyes as well as my own. Plus, truth be told, I simply love giving gifts. If gift-giving isn't your love language, find some other way to spoil your clients that's more inherent to who you are.

The 6 Steps to Social Media Marketing Your Weddings

Oftentimes we can feel behind the curveball when trying to figure out how to market our work, especially with weddings when the demographic we're trying to target is the one that changes the most rapidly.

If you're like me, you're in a constant marketing method flux trying to find out what works and what doesn't so that you can put food on your table. The truth of the situation is exactly how Gary Vaynerchuk put it in his great book, Jab Jab Jab Right Hook, "There is no time to mourn the past or feel sorry for ourselves, and there is no point in self-pity anyway."

As we market our businesses, we always have to keep moving forward. We have to keep up with what's happening in wedding and social trends, and we have to find new ways to get our names, business and work out there. Here are six ways you can do just that.

Instagram

Instagram is being harnessed by some of the biggest brand names out there like Anthropologie, Macy's and Coca-Cola. It's obviously a tool that big businesses are seeing the value in, and we should see the value in it too.

Luckily for us business owners and especially wedding business owners, Instagram is photo-based. Their target demographic is our target demographic, adults between the ages of 18 and 34. Many couples now have hashtags for their weddings. You can Instagram photos so that the bride and groom see them, and you can Instagram all their guests as well. Using Instagram should be part of our workflow as wedding business owners.

If you're not already using Instagram for your business, give it a try and just post one picture a week, preferably on a Sunday evening, as it's an active time for couples in the marrying age range. If you are currently using Instagram, make sure you're utilizing hashtags when you post. Use a 5-7 hashtags that are relevant to the photo, and ask your clients if they have a hashtag to insert as well. Be sure to check out one of the previous chapters for more details on Instagram posting. This is just a short summary!

Finally, make sure that you browse hashtags that are relevant to the clients you're looking for, such as #ring, #engaged and #wedding planning, and leave likes and comments (not spam comments, but real ones) on those photos. It'll help boost your following and get you seen by people who may not have encountered you otherwise.

TikTok

"Oh no, I'm not dancing!" That's the usual response I get when I mention business owners (or anyone) getting on TikTok.

They would be right, TikTok really did start, and still has, a bunch of dancing videos, but that's not all that's there. Since the COVID-19 pandemic in 2020, TikTok has become a huge social media platform now hosting every kind of creator and human being (actually and animals too) that wants to participate. It has marketing, it has humor and it absolutely 100% has couples getting married, with the majority of users being in the demographic just before marriage.

Long story short: get on it. Learn it if for nothing else than to see what your potential clients see and understand them better, gets the jokes and humor and trends that are all a part of it. Will it be around forever and have the longevity that platforms like Facebook and Instagram do, or will it be another Google plus? It doesn't matter. Your clients are there now. Go hang out with them.

Vendor Networking

Networking with your local vendors may not seem like social media, but it absolutely can be. With social media and vendors, you're looking to tap into their network of fans, and they're looking to tap into yours. There are 100 different creative ways you can cross-promote, so do what you're best at and get creative.

Some of the vendor networking I do that winds up on social media includes guest posting and creating mobile apps for them. With guest posting, a vendor and I can write blog articles for each other, usually informational and with their audience in mind. We post them and then blast about them on all of our social media outlets. This allows us to give valuable information to each of our networks while expanding our brands into them as well.

A fun new way I'm interacting with my local wedding vendors is to create an app for them using [Sticky Albums](). If you haven't used Sticky Albums yet, definitely give it a try as it's super easy to use and can create a lot of buzz, not only for your clients but for networking as well. Just today I created an app for a florist that I've worked with a few times, using his logo at the top and with my logo on the photos. I use photos that I have of the weddings we've shot together. It's a perfect way to give your vendors something special that won't break the bank or cost you much time, and they can easily share them via Facebook and to their network of potential clients. If you're not a photographer, you can still find a fun way to incorporate easy apps like this into your marketing plan and customer experience.

Facebook Advertising

You may think Facebook is going downhill and not where today's couples are, but it's still an extremely relevant social media platform for weddings. Everyone expects to see a couple's wedding photos posted online shortly after they get married, and that includes the generation above them (aka parents of the couple and their friends). I'm a proponent of doing that the night of the wedding, but even well after that, Facebook should still be used to post a preview or two of wedding images with your logo and website link in the description.

I want to highlight the advertising features of Facebook more than just it's general relevance to our industry. So many people are aggravated that the free marketing gravy train is over on Facebook and Instagram, and yes, that's disappointing. However, the paid advertising tool they have incorporated is quite powerful and should be taken advantage of. For countless years, one of marketers' main goals is to find out two things: first, what type of advertising works, and second, how we can hit our target audience. Facebook paid advertising helps you answer those two questions, no problem.

Because you can post an update and see (for free) the analytics of how it's being accepted by those who view it, it's Facebook's way of letting you know before you pay for it, which posts are successful and catching the viewer's eye. This is priceless information because no longer will you spend money on a direct mail piece with artwork that causes the receiver to simply throw it in the garbage. Now we know, ahead of spending money, what picture, phrasing or call to action gets the most response. When you find that, move to answering question two.

Facebook makes it beyond easy to hit your target audience, which for us wedding business owners is usually women between the ages of 25-32 (this varies depending on where you live in the country and the average marrying age of women there—so do your research on that), who are engaged and living in an area of the country or state that you service. All of these demographics are manageable within Facebook Ads, and you can target that already successful ad campaign directly to them. Or, you can upload a list of your past and current clients and create a look-a-like list. Booyah!

Facebook/Instagram advertising can get complicated, so it's not out of the question to outsource this. At the time of writing this book a good Facebook campaign manager costs roughly $1000 a month (plus the cost of ads), and the really good ones that'll incorporate a drip email sequence in for you can be a little higher up front, but well worth it. Check out https://creativecinc.sitedev.cc/ for one of my favorite marketing firms that can handle this for you from start to finish.

Pinterest

A client may say to you, "I found these pictures on Pinterest – can you take them at my wedding?" This doesn't have to be the only interaction you have with Pinterest. Pinterest is the wedding planning Mecca of the Internet right now, and with 68% of its users being female, you need to be there as a wedding professional.

Successful pins inspire and give ideas, and your photos should do the same. Consider making separate boards for things like "Wedding Cakes," "Bridal Shoes" and "Engagement Session Outfits." Make sure the photo links back to your blog or website. I like to have my logo on the photo as well, just in case.

Again, if Pinterest just seems like another social media task, don't worry, you can pin simultaneously using that EveryPost app I mentioned earlier as well. Oh, and you can schedule those posts ahead of time, too.

Get Published

One of the best things you can do for your social media is to have others talk about you. Getting published in online blogs and magazines is a great way to make this happen with very little effort on your part. As a side benefit, it'll also help boost your SEO by having link-backs to your website on so many other websites.

Getting published is not only for business owners with connections or those who have amazing photographs and have been in the business for years. Getting published is for business owners who capture interesting details at weddings (the #1 thing publishers are looking for) and who submit those photos to be considered for publication. It's as easy as that.

The easiest way to submit your work to be considered for publication is to use www.TwoBrightLights. It does take a little bit of time to do, but it's peanuts for the exposure that it can get you. Every time you have your work published, most publishers will post about it on social media, getting your name and photos in front of their network of couples. It's a win-win.

These are just six basic ideas to utilizing social media for your business, but marketing is endless. It's a game of experimentation and flowing with current trends. Take what I've given you, test it out, and tweak it until it fits with your business and clientele perfectly.

About the Author

VANESSA JOY

Vanessa Joy is a Canon Explorer of Light that has been an influential speaker in the community for over a decade. Starting her photographic journey in 1998, she has since branched into public speaking, earned five college degrees, received a PPA Photographic Craftsman degree, been named a WeddingWire Education Expert, sponsored by Canon, Profoto and Animoto, to name a few. Vanessa has spoken at almost every major convention and platform in the event industry such as CreativeLIVE, The Wedding School, Clickin' Moms, WPPI, ShutterFest, Imaging USA, Wedding MBA, WeddingWire World, MobileBeat, in addition to hosting personal workshops and numerous small business and photography conventions around the globe. Recognized for her talent and more so her business sense, her clients love working with her and industry peers love to learn from her tangible, informative and open-book style of teaching. Find her at www.VanessaJoy.com.